TEXTS AND STUDIES

CONTRIBUTIONS TO
BIBLICAL AND PATRISTIC LITERATURE

EDITED BY

J. ARMITAGE ROBINSON D.D.

HON. PH.D. GÖTTINGEN   HON. D.D. HALLE   HON. D.D. DUBLIN
HON. D.D. GLASGOW   HON. FELLOW OF CHRIST'S COLLEGE
DEAN OF WELLS

VOL. VIII.

No. 3. THE ODES OF SOLOMON

THE ODES OF SOLOMON

EDITED
WITH INTRODUCTION AND NOTES

BY

J. H. BERNARD, D.D.

HON. D.C.L. DURHAM   HON. D.D. ABERDEEN
BISHOP OF OSSORY, FERNS AND LEIGHLIN

Eugene, Oregon

Wipf and Stock Publishers
199 W 8th Ave, Suite 3
Eugene, OR 97401

The Odes of Solomon
By Bernard, J.H. and Robinson, J. Armitage
ISBN: 1-59244-837-2
Publication date 8/26/2004
Previously published by Cambridge, 1912

PREFACE

THE remains of the Christian literature of the second century which have come down to us are scanty, and are, for the most part, devoid of merit as literature, while deeply interesting and valuable to the student of Christian origins. The *Odes of Solomon*, the most recent addition to our collection of early Christian books, are specially welcome, not only for the light which they throw upon primitive beliefs, but because of their literary excellence. Whoever the author may have been, he had something of the poetical *afflatus*; nor would it be easy to find Christian poems of any age which strike a higher spiritual note. 'Solomon' is the first Christian poet in order of time, and not the least in order of inspiration.

The *Odes* have attracted many editors since their publication, but no editor has done fuller justice to their poetry and their spirituality than Dr Rendel Harris, who discovered them. It has not been my purpose to dwell upon the many beauties of thought and expression which the Odes reveal to the student; for Dr Harris has illustrated these with such sympathy and appreciation that no other edition than his is needed, from the point of view of a lover of sacred poetry.

My task has been a more prosaic one, namely to examine the Odes with the view of discovering the habits of religious life and thought which they presuppose. In order to explain their phraseology, I have quoted freely from the early theological writers of

the Eastern Church; and I believe that the parallelisms in though\
and language which they present are so numerous and precise as
to make it certain that the *Odes* are built up on a substructure of
baptismal ritual and doctrine. I have ventured to suggest that
they actually were Hymns of the Catechumens, or Hymns of the
newly baptized taught to Catechumens as part of their instruction.
Whatever may be thought of the arguments which have been
marshalled in support of this opinion, it cannot be doubted, I think,
that the Odist has in his mind the distinctive beliefs which the
early Church entertained as to baptism and its privileges.

It may seem to some that such an interpretation of the *Odes*
robs them of their peculiar interest and beauty. They are thus
no longer private songs of a devout spirit, rejoicing in "the joy of
the Lord," untrammelled by any fetters of dogma, but they are the
hymns of the Christian community, fully developed and organised,
their phrases deliberately chosen so as to illustrate the doctrines
of baptism. But the truth is that it is difficult for later genera-
tions of the Church to whom baptism does not constitute the
conscious crisis of the Christian life to appreciate the heights
which these Odes reach. Overpowering as are the gains of Infant
Baptism, we learn here something of what is lost by it to the
Christian experience. We can understand the lofty spirituality of
the *Odes*, but we find it hard to associate this with the joy of the
newly baptized. Yet nothing is clearer in the records of the early
Eastern Church than the exalted place which was assigned to
baptism as the great crisis in the history of the soul. The *Odes* do
not differ in this respect from Ephraim's baptismal hymns; their
distinctiveness is not in their doctrinal implications, but rather in
the beauty and dignity of the language which the singer employs
to express his hope and his rejoicing.

And if, as I believe may be said, these Odes were primarily
intended for the edification of the Catechumens, we can understand how valuable they would be, as bringing out the spiritual

aspects of the new life to which baptism admitted the neophyte. The risk of superstition and of interpretations of the baptismal act which reduce it to a magical performance, has always been a real danger among simple people; and hymns such as these would serve to turn their thoughts to the higher and more spiritual side of the Christian initiation. Where books were not available for the generality, this poetical form of instruction, learnt by heart, would be of great value—a permanent gift of spiritual help stored in the memory.

JOHN OSSORY.

THE PALACE, KILKENNY.
Eastertide, 1912.

CONTENTS

		PAGE
PREFACE	. . . .	i
INTRODUCTION	. . . .	
Sect. 1.	Previous Editions	1
2.	Various theories as to the Odes	2
3.	The evidence of Lactantius	4
4.	Silence of early Fathers	6
5.	Pistis Sophia	7
6.	The original language of the Odes . . .	9
7.	The Lists of Sacred Books	11
8.	The Odes cited as Scripture	13
9.	The attribution of the Odes to Solomon . .	14
10.	The Testamentum Domini	16
11.	Cyril of Jerusalem	18
12.	Baptismal hymns in the early Church . .	19
13.	Topics not mentioned in the Odes . . .	22
14.	The Disciplina Arcani	23
15.	Christian doctrine in the Odes	25
16.	Allusions to Holy Scripture	26
17.	The Odes not Gnostic	28
18.	The Logos Doctrine in the Odes	30
19.	The Baptism of Christ and the Descent into Hades .	32
20.	The interchange of speakers in the Odes . .	39
21.	The "Adversaries" of the Odist	40
22.	The Unity of Authorship	41
23.	Conclusion	42
TRANSLATION AND NOTES	. . . .	45
INDEX TO PATRISTIC PARALLELS CITED IN THE NOTES	. . .	133

INTRODUCTION

§ 1. *Previous Editions.*

THE "Odes of Solomon" have nothing in common with the "Psalms of Solomon," except the name of the supposed author. The "Psalms of Solomon" are a collection of 18 Psalms of the Pharisees, originally written in the middle of the last century before Christ. They have been edited more than once in a Greek version, extant in several manuscripts, and provide valuable information as to the hopes and aspirations of later Judaism.

Up to the year 1909 all that was known of *Odes* as distinct from *Psalms* bearing the name of Solomon was that they were mentioned in two catalogues of extra canonical books, that five of them were cited in a Gnostic treatise entitled *Pistis Sophia*, and that Lactantius makes a single quotation from them.

In 1909 Dr Rendel Harris published the text of the "Odes and Psalms of Solomon" from a Syriac manuscript in his possession which was probably written in the sixteenth century (H). The manuscript contained originally 42 Odes followed by 18 Psalms; but, as both beginning and end are lost, it supplies no title for the collection, and the text of Odes i and ii, and of Psalm xviii, is missing. Harris at once identified the later pieces with the "Psalms of Solomon" which were already well known to scholars in Greek; and he was not slow to discover that the earlier pieces included the five "Odes" which are extant in the Coptic *Pistis Sophia*. It was thus apparent that he had recovered the collection, almost in its entirety, of the long-lost "Odes of Solomon"; and the publication of their text aroused the keenest interest among scholars. A German edition (without the Syriac text) was published in 1910 in the *Texte und Untersuchungen*, consisting of a translation by J. Flemming and a commentary by Harnack; and another German edition by Staerk and Ungnad soon followed. Innumerable articles appeared in theological magazines, and a French version by Labourt with notes by Batiffol was issued in 1911. The latest edition is that by H. Grimme, who has translated the Odes into Hebrew, which he believes to have been the original language. More recently still, Professor Burkitt[1] discovered a second manuscript (N) among the Nitrian collection in the British Museum (Add. 14538), of the tenth century or earlier. This contains the Syriac text of the Odes from xvii 7 to the end, and of portions of the Psalms, which follow the Odes as in H.

It is not often that a discovery of the kind has attracted so much attention; but the enigmas presented by the Odes are so puzzling that the solutions put forward by successive editors and commentators have been various and contradictory.

§ 2. *Various theories as to the Odes.*

Harris regards the Odes (or most of them) as the work of a Jewish Christian, writing at the end of the first century. He believes them to have been written originally in Greek, and he treats them as private poems, breathing the spirit of an exalted mysticism, without sacramental reference. He lays stress upon the unity of style which they exhibit, and counts them as the work of a single author.

Harnack considers that the Odes in their original form were purely Jewish, and explains the Christian allusions that they contain as due to a Christian editor. The original work was composed (he holds) while the Temple at Jerusalem was still standing, a conclusion which is derived from his interpretation of the opening sentences of Ode iv; and he fixes the date of the Christian interpolator and of the Odes in their present form at c. 100 A.D.

Grimme, following on Harnack's lines, finds the clue to the Odes in the hypothesis of a Hebrew original[2], and boldly distinguishes the Christian interpolations from the *Urtext.* He

[1] See *Journal of Theological Studies* for April 1912; from this article I have derived my knowledge of the readings of N.
[2] See p. 9 below.

thinks that the original may be as early as 100 B.C. and could not, in any case, be later than 30 A.D. The Christian editor he would place somewhat later than Harnack does.

Dr Menzies[1] put forward the view that the Odes are really Jewish throughout (although he did not explain in detail passages like Ode xxxi 3 f.), and he called them *Psalms of the Proselytes*. He argued with much force that the Odist speaks again and again of newly acquired spiritual privileges.

The theory of an interpolated text is one which ought only to be adopted as a *dernier ressort*[2]. If the text is self-explanatory without any such hypothesis, then the hypothesis becomes unnecessary and, as it has no external evidence in its favour, it has no claim to acceptance. In October, 1910, I printed an article in the *Journal of Theological Studies*, in which I put forward a different hypothesis from any of the foregoing, viz. that the Odes were Christian throughout, and that the numerous allusions which they contain to baptismal doctrine and to the Eastern ritual of baptism, indicate that they are Hymns of the Baptised, comparable to the Hymns of Ephraim Syrus[3].

This view is comparable to that of Menzies in that it takes account, as significant, of the continual stress laid by the Odist upon the privileges of Divine grace which have lately been placed within his reach; but it is, of course, at variance with the view that the Odes are Jewish, as it is equally at variance with Harnack's theory of interpolation, and with Harris's interpretation of them as the poems of a non-sacramental mystic.

My aim in this edition is to exhibit in detail the evidence for the baptismal character of the Odist's language. Whether the

[1] *The Interpreter*, Oct. 1910.

[2] Clemen argues against Harnack's interpolation theory, in the *Theologische Rundschau*, Jan. 1911; and Dom Connolly has also shewn convincingly the unity of the Odes in a valuable essay in the *Journal of Theological Studies* for Jan. 1912.

[3] Dr Harris pointed out to me in a private communication in December, 1910, that G. Diettrich had suggested, as far back as May, 1910, that the Odes contained references to baptismal customs; but, so far as I know, he has not followed this up. Diettrich held with Harnack that two *strata* might be detected in the Odes, one Jewish of an Essene character, and the other Christian but of a heretical sort. (*Die Reformation*, May 8, June 5, Aug. 7, Aug. 14, 1910.) Professor Kirsopp Lake also called attention to the baptismal character of the Odes in the *Theologisch Tijdschrift* for Nov. 1910, but he did not discuss the question at length.

Odes are hymns intended to be sung by persons who have recently received baptism, or by catechumens who are preparing for it, is a question to which we shall recur. The conclusion which I have reached as to date is that the Odes were composed in their present form in the second half of the second century (150–190 A.D.); that they are Asiatic in origin and express the beliefs and hopes of Eastern Christianity; and that they were probably written at the first in Syriac, although upon this point I do not venture to offer any confident opinion. That they were intended for public recitation, rather than for private use; and that they are orthodox in intention and in language, is, I believe, capable of demonstration[1].

§ 3. *The Evidence of Lactantius.*

The point from which we must start in an investigation of the date of the Odes is the citation of Ode xix 6 by Lactantius in his *Divine Institutes*, and also in his *Epitome* of that work. His words are: "Salomon in ode undevicesima ita dicit: Infirmatus est uterus virginis et accepit fetum et gravata est, et facta est in multa miseratione mater virgo[2]." He introduces the same quotation in a similar way in the *Epitome*: "apud Salomonem ita scriptum est."

Lactantius was a learned man, a native of Africa, who was for some years a teacher of rhetoric in Nicomedia. He left Nicomedia for Gaul about the year 305, and the *Divine Institutes* was published not later than 310[3].

Harris points out[4] that when Lactantius quotes Greek books, such as the Sibylline Oracles, he quotes in Greek and does not offer a translation, whereas he quotes Ode xix 6 in Latin. Hence Harris concludes that a Latin version of the Odes was current before 310. This inference is somewhat precarious. We have no trace, outside the writings of Lactantius, of any acquaintance with the Odes of Solomon among Latin writers. As we shall see, they were known in the East, but we cannot say that they were known

---

[1] Harris prints a useful bibliography of the literature that has gathered round the Odes, at p. ix of his second edition (1911).
[2] *Div. Inst.* iv. 12.
[3] See Lawlor, *Hermathena*, 1903, p. 459.   [4] *Introd.* p. 9.

in the West. Lactantius, who was a man of wide erudition, may be supposed to have learnt of their existence during his residence in Nicomedia. It is even possible that he knew them only in Syriac (which is our own case), or from the report of Syriac scholars; and in that case he would naturally quote them in the vernacular, as we do. We have, indeed, no proof that he understood the Syriac language, but we must not assume that he was wholly ignorant of it. The difficulty as to the rendering which he gives of the verse he quotes (see note on *infirmatus*, Ode xix 6), may have been due to his imperfect acquaintance with Syriac. But even if he knew Ode xix 6 in a Greek form, we cannot conclude with certainty that he must have quoted it in Greek, because he preferred to transcribe the Sibylline verses in their original language. In no age have authors been so precisely consistent in their methods.

Lactantius knew the Odes as a collection, for he indicates the number of the Ode from which he quotes. "Solomon in ode undevicesima ita dicit" is the phrase with which he introduces Ode xix 6. He does not quote, that is, from hearsay, but writes with a book before him. Lactantius is fond of quoting from pagan and non-canonical writings, and the Odes would have been quite in his line of study.

It is plain too that he not only knew the Odes but knew them as Odes which bore the name of Solomon. There is nothing in his manner of quoting Ode xix 6 which would differentiate it from Scripture. He may have been unconscious that he was quoting from a non-canonical work. In Pichon's study of Lactantius[1], it is pointed out that his Bible quotations do not exhibit any special familiarity with the Old Testament—he only became a Christian while living in Nicomedia—and Pichon thinks that he may have got them from a collection of *Testimonia* like Cyprian's. If this be a well-grounded opinion, we can understand how Lactantius, alone among the Fathers, Eastern or Western, could have made the mistake of quoting the Odes as genuine Solomonic prophecy. He did not accurately know the limits or the contents of the Old Testament. Other Fathers may have known the Odes, and

---

[1] *Lactance*, par R. Pichon (1901). Lawlor (l.c.) does not accept all of Pichon's reasoning as to this point.

probably some of them did, but they knew that they were not Scripture, and so they did not quote them.

The evidence, then, of Lactantius amounts to this—that the Odes were known and were ascribed to Solomon before the year 305 in the district of Nicomedia. We cannot be sure of the existence of a Latin version, nor even whether Lactantius had access to them in Greek or in Syriac, but we can be sure that he counted them to be genuine writings of Solomon.

§ 4. *Silence of early Fathers.*

On the other hand, Basil of Caesarea, half a century later, seems to say that he only knew of three books bearing the name of Solomon, viz. Proverbs, Ecclesiastes and Canticles: τρεῖς τὰς πάσας ἔγνωμεν πραγματείας τοῦ σοφωτάτου Σολομῶντος[1]. In like manner Philo of Carpasia (another fourth century writer) in his Preface to the Canticles betrays no knowledge of any ᾠδαί ascribed to Solomon, while he mentions the Song of Moses, of Isaiah, and so forth.

Even more important is the witness of Origen, who seems also to be unaware of the existence of "Odes of Solomon." He discusses, in his Prologue to the Canticles[2], the meaning of the title "the Song of Songs, which is Solomon's," and infers that the use of the singular verb implies that the canonical piece alone is by Solomon, and that it is not to be regarded as one survivor out of many which Solomon wrote. "Sed nos quomodo recipiemus huiusmodi intelligentiam, cum neque ecclesia Dei ulla extrinsecus Salomonis cantica legenda susceperit: neque apud Hebraeos... aliquid praeter hos tres libellos Salomonis[3], qui et apud nos sunt, amplius habeatur in canone?" The other opinion he puts thus: "Ex his ergo quinque milibus[4] canticis volunt videri hoc unum esse canticum, quod habemus: sed usquequo vel ubi cantata sint, non solum ad usum, sed ne ad notitiam quidem pervenit ecclesiarum Dei." Even, he says, if fragments of them were to be found in the apocryphal books, they would remain apocryphal and without

---

[1] Hom. XII. *in principium Proverbiorum* 1.
[2] Written at Athens about 240: Lommatzsch XIV. 324 f.
[3] *i.e.* Proverbs, Ecclesiastes, and Canticles.   [4] Sc. 1005.

authority. His language is prolix, but it would be disingenuous if he was aware of the existence of "Odes of Solomon" which had currency in Christian circles, either Catholic or heretical.

These passages do not prove, be it observed, that our Odes were entirely unknown to Basil, Philo of Carpasia, and Origen; but only that, if they were in use in the Churches known to these writers, they did not bear the name of Solomon, as they did in the circles in which Lactantius moved[1].

§ 5. *Pistis Sophia*.

We have next to observe that five of the Odes are cited *in extenso* in the fantastic Gnostic treatise known as *Pistis Sophia*, which is extant in Coptic. Odes i, v, vi, xxii and xxv are quoted and given a Gnostic interpretation in this book. Not only are they cited, but they are cited as Solomon's, and are made the subject of comment as if they were canonical Scripture. ἐπροφήτευσε *per Salomonem* is the phrase which introduces them, the subject of the verb being *vis luminis*. No difference can be observed between the manner in which the Odes and the canonical Psalms are treated.

Pistis Sophia is an obscure book, and it would be rash to speak with confidence about it. Its latest editor is Schmidt[2], who holds that it is probably of Egyptian derivation, but that the Gnosticism which inspired it is that of the sects who had their origin in Syria, and that it may be ascribed to the latter half of the third century. It would be to go beyond the evidence to profess to date it within twenty or thirty years. It may be as early as 270 or it may be as late as 290 or even 300. The information which it provides as to the Odes is specially important in two respects. First, it represents *Syrian* Gnosticism and therefore it may be concluded that the Odes were known in Syria when the book was compiled. And secondly, the Odes are quoted as on a par with the canonical Psalms. They are allegorised and commented on just as if they were Scripture, and this points to the conviction of the compilers

---

[1] The arguments used above would apply equally well to the "Psalms of Solomon."

[2] *Koptische Gnostische Schriften* (1905).

that they were truly Solomon's. The evidence of *Pistis Sophia*, like the evidence of Lactantius, points to the fact that the Odes had a vogue as Scripture, or at any rate as possessing the authority which belonged to Solomon's name, as early as 270 A.D. or thereabouts.

We cannot tell for how long a period the Odes had been in circulation before they acquired this authoritative position. Some considerable time must have elapsed between their compilation and their acceptance by Lactantius, the Catholic scholar, and by the heretical author of *Pistis Sophia*. But whether this interval was one of a century, or a century and a half, external evidence does not tell us. We may be sure that the Odes were in existence before 250 A.D., and it seems probable that we might say before 200 A.D.; but for any closer determination of their date we shall be driven back on the internal evidence of their contents.

The five Odes which are extant in *Pistis Sophia* in Coptic are accessible in Schmidt's able translation of that curious and repulsive treatise. He provided a revised rendering for Harnack and Flemming's edition: and more recently these five Odes have been translated afresh into English and their Coptic text compared with the Syriac, by W. H. Worrell[1]. I have cited the more important Coptic variants from Mr Worrell's edition[2].

That the Coptic renderings of our Odes in *Pistis Sophia* are derived from a Greek version is probable, although it cannot be pronounced certain. The Coptic Odes are interspersed, indeed, with a few Greek words; but that is true of all Coptic literature, for Coptic is a language with a scanty vocabulary and frequently borrows from Greek. Even if the Coptic Odes were translated from a Syriac or Aramaic original, we should probably find some Greek words used. What can be affirmed with certainty is that

---

[1] Mr Worrell compares the Syriac (S) with the Coptic text (C), and also with the text of the Gnostic hymn (T) which the author of *Pistis Sophia* derives from C. He notes some differences between T and C in the text of Ode v., and observes that S sometimes agrees with T as against C. Hence he derives the conclusion that these Odes were extant originally in two forms, a Gnostic (T) and an orthodox (C), and that the Syriac (S) through its ancestor was affected by T. But this is to build up a theory on very slight evidence; that the Gnostic hymns and the orthodox hymns circulated side by side is not probable.

[2] *Journal of Theological Studies*, October, 1911, pp. 28 ff.

the Odes were extant in Greek in the sixth century, as we shall see further on[1], and a Greek version may very well lie behind those of them which are preserved in Coptic.

But attention must now be called to the significant fact that the extant Coptic Odes vary remarkably in text from the same Odes preserved in Syriac. The variants are too considerable to allow us to suppose that they are altogether due to the ordinary mistakes of scribes: and this has an important bearing upon the question next to be considered, namely, the original language of the Odes. Were they originally written in Greek, or were they written in a Semitic language? If they were Greek at the first, we must postulate two versions of the Greek, one lying behind the Coptic and another lying behind the Syriac of Odes v, vi, xxii, xxv.

§ 6. *The original language of the Odes.*

Harris examined this question in his *editio princeps* (pp. 37 ff.), and he concluded that the original language was Greek. Comparing the Syriac Psalms of Solomon with their known Greek text, he found that many of the readings of the Syriac were explicable on the hypothesis that the Syriac translator was working from the Greek; and he suggested that the same might be said of the text of the Odes, which preceded the Psalms in his unique manuscript. But he did not provide any complete proof of this in his interesting dissertation (pp. 46, 47): for his ingenious explanation of the variations between the Coptic and Syriac texts of Ode vi 16 (see note) is not satisfying. It is not necessary to suppose that the textual history of the *Odes of Solomon* is identical with the textual history of the *Psalms of Solomon*, with which they are associated.

Following up a suggestion of Harnack's, Professor Grimme[2] has worked out a different conclusion. His theory is that behind both Syriac and Coptic lies a text in Biblical Hebrew, which he holds to be the language in which the Odes were originally composed. He has translated the extant Syriac into Hebrew, and he finds signs of an alphabetical arrangement in his reconstructed Hebrew

---
[1] p. 11.
[2] *Die Oden Salomos Syrisch-Hebräisch-Deutsch*, von H. Grimme (Heidelberg, 1911).

text. Thus Odes i[1], iv, v begin with the Hebrew letter א (אדני, אין, אודך being the opening words); Odes vi, vii begin with ב; Odes viii, ix with ג; Odes x—xiii with ה; Odes xiv—xxi with כ (to establish this it has to be assumed that Ode xviii has lost its first line); Odes xxii, xxiii with ס; Odes xxiv—xxvi with נ; Ode xxvii with פ; Ode xxviii with כ (not ק, as we should expect); Odes xxix—xxxiii with ש. After this point, the acrostic arrangement is interrupted, and Grimme offers various suggestions to explain the failure of the series. The theory is very ingenious, but it has large gaps. Some initial letters do not occur at all in the acrostic scheme, and the explanations of its disappearance after Ode xxxiv, which the author of the theory offers, do not carry conviction.

Grimme proceeds to argue that the original language must be Biblical Hebrew, and not Aramaic (which would fit the acrostic scheme equally well), (1) because he finds in the double meanings of certain Hebrew words the explanation of some difficulties in the extant Syriac text, and (2) because of the metrical system which he finds in the reconstructed Hebrew. Under (1) the best instances are: אחיהם means "their like" rather than "their brother" in Ode xxviii 14; אפס may be "nothing" rather than "not" in Ode xix 8; חפה means "bridal canopy" rather than "bridal couch" in Ode xlii 11; but even these are not conclusive. As to (2) the laws of Hebrew Metric are hardly well enough known as yet to build so much on them as Professor Grimme does.

Nevertheless, and making all deductions, Grimme's arguments tend to support the theory of a Semitic original for the Odes—not necessarily or probably in Biblical Hebrew, but in Aramaic or even in Syriac. It has not yet been established that the Syriac manuscripts do not contain the original text, however corrupted in the course of centuries. As we shall see, the subject-matter of the Odes has a Syrian or Palestinian flavour, and it may well be that their original language was Syriac rather than Greek.

The coincidences between the language of the Odes and many phrases in the hymns of Ephraim Syrus, of which something will be said further on[2], have been used in a recent article by Harris[3]

---

[1] Ode ii and the beginning of Ode iii are missing.
[2] p. 20 and notes *passim.*   [3] *Expositor*, December, 1911.

in an attempt to demonstrate that Ephraim knew and used the Odes. If this could be established, it would provide another argument for a Syriac original, or at any rate for an early Syriac version; for it is in Ephraim's Syriac writings that the parallels are most abundant. But without accepting the theory of Ephraim's literary dependence upon the Odes—for the similarities, as will be shewn, may be due to a common relationship to the baptismal ritual—the tone and temper of Ephraim's hymns is so like that of the *Odes of Solomon*, that we may conclude that they were composed in a similar environment, *i.e.* that the Odes are Syrian in origin. And if this be so, they were probably written at first in Syriac[1].

In any case, it is certain that a Greek translation of them was in existence at a later time, and we now proceed to deal with the evidence for this.

§ 7. *The Lists of Sacred Books.*

There is an explicit mention of the Odes in the sixth century catalogue of Sacred Books, entitled the *Synopsis Sacrae Scripturae*, which goes (incorrectly) under the name of Athanasius[2]. After an enumeration of the canonical books of the Old Testament, Pseudo-Athanasius proceeds to say (col. 239): ἐκτὸς δὲ τούτων εἰσὶ πάλιν ἕτερα βιβλία τῆς παλαιᾶς διαθήκης, οὐ κανονιζόμενα μέν, ἀναγινωσκόμενα δὲ μόνον τοῖς κατηχουμένοις. This sentence is very similar to (though not identical with) a sentence of the genuine Athanasius in his list of Sacred Books[3], and both writers then proceed to mention the books of Wisdom, Ecclesiasticus, Esther, Judith, and Tobit. But Pseudo-Athanasius adds at a later point (col. 432):

Μακκαβαϊκὰ βιβλία δ'
Πτολεμαϊκά[4]
ψαλμοὶ καὶ ᾠδὴ Σολομῶντος
Σωσάννα.

[1] W. R. Newbold thinks that Bardaisan may have been their author (*Journal of Bibl. Lit.* vol. xxx. ii. pp. 161 ff.); but I am not convinced by the arguments he has adduced.
[2] It is printed in Migne, *P.G.* xxviii. 283 ff.
[3] *Ep. fest.* 39 (Migne, *P.G.* xxvi. 1437).
[4] We need not delay upon the interpretation of this entry.

ψαλμοὶ Σολομῶντος in this entry represents the Jewish "Psalms of Solomon"; and ᾠδή (no doubt a mistake for ᾠδαί) represents our Odes. We do not know in what locality this catalogue of Pseudo-Athanasius originated or had circulation; but it is certainly Eastern, not Western. The entry shews that the Odes of Solomon were placed on a par with the Psalms of Solomon, among the books just outside the Canon of the Old Testament, in the church where the catalogue was originally composed.

Our next witness is of a similar character. The *Stichometry* of Nicephorus is a list of Scriptural books reduced to its present form, according to Zahn's judgment[1], at Jerusalem about the year 850. The second part of the list runs as follows:

ὅσαι ἀντιλέγονται καὶ οὐκ ἐκκλησιάζονται
    Μακκαβαϊκὰ γ'. στίχ. ,ϛτ'
    Σοφία Σολομῶντος στίχ. ,αρ'
    Σοφία υἱοῦ τοῦ Σιρὰχ στίχ. ,βω'
    ψαλμοὶ καὶ ᾠδαὶ Σολομῶντος στίχ. ,βρ'
    Ἐσθὴρ στίχ. ,τν'
    Ἰουδὶθ στίχ. ,αψ'
    Σωσάννα στίχ. ,φ'
    Τωβίτ, ὁ καὶ Τωβίας στίχ. ,ψ'

Here the Psalms and Odes are given a higher place in the list, on account of their attribution to Solomon, immediately after Wisdom and Ecclesiasticus. Psalms and Odes together make 2100 στίχοι or verses, and Harris has calculated that, as other lists in which the Psalms alone are mentioned set them down as filling 950 στίχοι, this leaves 1150 στίχοι for the Odes. That gives us just the right proportion as to length between the Psalms, which are well known, and the new Syriac Odes. Thus there can be no doubt that the Odes which the *Stichometry* of Nicephorus mentions are those which have been recently recovered by Harris from the Syriac.

It is to be borne in mind that both Pseudo-Athanasius and the author of this *Stichometry* may have been copying, without

---

[1] *N.T. Kanon*, II. i. 295 n.

any close scrutiny of its contents, an older list[1], and that thus their catalogues do not prove that the Odes were really well known in their respective localities in the sixth and ninth centuries respectively. All that they prove beyond doubt is that the title had been preserved, and also a correct tradition as to the length of the book which contained them. Books continued to be mentioned in Scriptural lists long after they ceased to be transcribed as Scripture; and it may have been so in this case.

§ 8. *The Odes cited as Scripture.*

The question now presents itself, How did our Odes come to be quoted as Scripture by Lactantius and the author of *Pistis Sophia*, and how did they come to be included in Scriptural lists? The answer which seems most probable is that they were used in early times as Church hymns, and hence were reckoned as ᾠδαί, of the same character as the recognised ᾠδαί, the Song of Moses, the Song of Hannah and the rest.

The Codex Alexandrinus (A) gives at the end of the canonical Psalter fourteen of these ᾠδαί, which were in constant liturgical use in the Eastern Church; viz. Exod. xv 1—19, Deut. xxxii 1—43, 1 Sam. ii 1—10, Isa. xxvi 9—20, Jonah ii 3—10, Hab. iii 1—19, Isa. xxxviii 10—20, The Prayer of Manasseh, Dan. iii 26—45, Dan. iii 52—88, Luke i 46—55, Luke ii 29—32, Luke i 68—79, and the *Gloria in Excelsis* (the morning hymn of the Church). The Psalters of Verona (R) and of Zürich (T) add some of these Odes to the Psalms of David in like fashion. One of these pieces, at any rate, viz. *Gloria in Excelsis*, is not Scriptural, and yet it was transcribed as Scripture along with the other ᾠδαί by the scribes of A and T. No doubt T is a liturgical Psalter, and probably the archetype of this part of A was the same[2]. But the juxtaposition of these Odes with the canonical Psalms in a manuscript of the authority of Codex Alexandrinus shews how

---

[1] It has been pointed out to me by the General Editor that ψαλμοί καὶ ᾠδή Σολομῶντος is the entry not only in the List of Pseudo-Athanasius, but also in two MSS. of the *Stichometry* of Nicephorus (see Montfaucon, *Bibl. Coislin.* p. 204, and Zahn, *N.T. Kanon*, II. 299). That we should find ᾠδή for ᾠδαί in both lists is an indication (*valeat quantum*) of a common original from which they were copied.

[2] See Swete, *The O.T. in Greek*, II. p. ix.

readily pieces which had become familiar by ecclesiastical use would assume Scriptural rank. If it should appear on investigation that the Odes of Solomon were used in the public offices of the Church, we can understand how they would come to be quoted and transcribed, by those who did not make too critical distinctions, as on a par with the "Psalms of David."

The fact that confusion was caused by the use of non-canonical hymns is clear from the prohibition of the Council of Laodicea (about 363 A.D.). Canon LIX. provides ὅτι οὐ δεῖ ἰδιωτικοὺς ψαλμοὺς λέγεσθαι ἐν τῇ ἐκκλησίᾳ, οὐδὲ ἀκανόνιστα βιβλία, ἀλλὰ μόνα τὰ κανονικὰ τῆς παλαιᾶς καὶ καινῆς διαθήκης. Two commentators in the twelfth century[1] said that the "private psalms" referred to in this Canon were reputed to be by Solomon. This may or may not be the precise reference of the Council's prohibition—it is more applicable to the *Odes* than to the *Psalms* which bear Solomon's name—but, at any rate, the necessity for the Canon shews that non-canonical hymns were being used in the Church of Asia Minor in the fourth century.

§ 9. *The attribution of the Odes to Solomon.*

The title "the Odes of Solomon" has as yet received no adequate explanation from the commentators; and perhaps no certain answer can be given to the question, Why was Solomon regarded as their author?

It might be thought that the attribution of them to his authorship is due to a mere confusion, and it is conceivable that the mistake arose in some such way as the following. The so-called *Psalms of Solomon* are found in certain MSS. of the LXX. among the other Solomonic books, canonical and deuterocanonical. They are not found in Codex Alexandrinus (A), but they are mentioned at the end of the Catalogue in that MS., and this might have been the case in other MSS. Now the entry ψαλμοὶ Σολομῶντος would naturally be supplemented by the addition of ᾠδαί or καὶ ᾠδαί, if Odes (whether those before us or the Canonical Odes) followed in the text. And ψαλμοὶ Σολομῶντος καὶ ᾠδαί might

---

[1] Zonaras and Balsamon. See Ryle and James, *Psalms of the Pharisees*, pp. xxiii., xxiv.

easily be corrupted by subsequent transcribers into ψαλμοὶ καὶ ᾠδαὶ Σολομῶντος, the actual entry in the Catalogues of Pseudo-Athanasius and Nicephorus. This hypothesis would provide a possible explanation of the title "Odes of Solomon" attaching itself to hymns, which originally were composed without any thought of Solomon the Wise King. There is, however, no evidence for this conjecture, and it is undeniable that all the allusions to these Odes which have been traced describe them as Odes *of Solomon*. The Psalms of Solomon achieved a place just outside the margin of canonicity, because they were mistakenly believed to be by Solomon himself, and it is natural to think the same of the Odes. It was because they bore the name of Solomon—so it may be urged with much plausibility—that they were placed in the Biblical lists. Why was he supposed to be their author?

That Solomon composed 1005 "Odes" is the statement of 1 Kings iv 32[1]. And perhaps a sufficient explanation of our problem is that, inasmuch as Solomon was known to have written Odes, these Odes, familiar from their use in public worship, took on his name. No good reason can be assigned for the title "Psalms of Solomon" which the Psalms of the Pharisees acquired[2], and perhaps it is not necessary to seek any more exact explanation in the case of the Odes. If we permitted ourselves to speculate we might recall the application of the mystic "Song of Songs" (ᾆσμα ᾀσμάτων) to the Church and its privileges, and find here a reason why the Odes of the Baptized should bear Solomon's name. Or, again, Solomon's authority over the demoniacal powers of evil was a Jewish belief that lingered long in Christendom, and it is possible that the virtue of "Solomon's Seal" was associated by Christian simplicity with that of the seal of baptism. But we cannot prove that it was so, and thus the traditional title of the

---

[1] The LXX. of 1 Kings viii 53 speaks of a βιβλίον τῆς ᾠδῆς from which a poetical fragment (cp. 1 Kings viii 12, 13) is extracted. But this is probably a reference to the Book of Jashar (הַיָּשָׁר read as הַשִּׁיר); cp. Driver, *Introd. to O.T.* p. 182.

[2] Ryle and James say of these Psalms: "That the remainder of Solomon's writings might have included the present collection [*i.e.* the Psalms of the Pharisees] would seem to an uncritical age, accustomed to the production of pseudepigraphic works, to constitute a very probable supposition" (*The Psalms of the Pharisees*, p. lxi). We may say the same of the Odes.

Odes remains a problem as yet unsolved, on any hypothesis of their origin[1].

§ 10. *The Testamentum Domini.*

In the Morning Office described in the Syriac *Testamentum Domini* we find the following rubric: "Let them sing psalms and four hymns of praise: one by Moses, and of Solomon, and of the other prophets[2]." No doubt, the "psalms" are the Psalms of David, and the "hymns of praise" of Moses and the prophets are the Old Testament Canticles[3]—the ᾠδαί of the Eastern Church—which are appended (as has been pointed out) to some manuscripts of the LXX. But the "hymn of praise" of Solomon has not hitherto been identified. The canonical psalms ascribed to Solomon would come under the general description "psalms," and the Song of Songs is out of the question here, as quite unsuitable, both from its length and its nature, for singing in public worship. It is natural to think that we have here mention of our "Odes of Solomon." They are similar in character to the canonical ᾠδαί, being "hymns of praise," and are of appropriate length.

There are other references to these "hymns of praise" in the *Testamentum Domini* which would suit this identification. In the Maundy Thursday Office[4] we have the direction: "Let the little boys say spiritual psalms and hymns of praise by the light of the lamp. Let all the people respond *Hallelujah* to the psalm and to the chant sung together, with one accord, with voices in harmony." This is a remarkable rubric. The liturgical acclamation *Hallelujah* or *Alleluia* was a feature of the Temple worship among the Jews, as we know from the "Hallelujah Psalms" (cxiii—cxviii), and it was taken over into Christian worship, being regularly used from the fifth or sixth century onwards at the Paschal season. But mention of it is rare in Ante Nicene writers[5],

---

[1] See p. 23 below and also on Ode i. [2] I. 26.

[3] Viz. Exod. xv 1—21; Deut. xxxii 1—43; 1 Sam. ii 1—10; Isa. v 1—9, xxvi 9—20, xxxviii 10—20; Jonah ii 3—10; Hab. iii 2—19; the Prayer of Manasseh; Dan. iii 26—45 and *Benedicite*.

[4] II. 11.

[5] Tertullian, *de Orat.* 27, is one of the very few instances. See Cabrol, *s.v.* "Alleluia" in *Dict. d'Archéologie Chrétienne*, i. 1231.

and the rubric which I have cited from the *Testamentum Domini* shews that its use is by no means a matter of course. It occurs in two anthems, for Epiphany and for the Feast of St John Baptist, preserved in a Fayoum papyrus[1]; and Pseudo-Dionysius tells us that it was used at the Benediction of the baptismal chrism. That is, the early Eastern notices of *Alleluia* in the Church associate it with baptismal joy, rather than with the festal season which followed Easter. And in the Syriac baptismal rites of a later date, it is frequently associated with anthems[2].

Now all the "Odes of Solomon" end with *Hallelujah*. This shews clearly that they are not private poems, but that they were intended for liturgical use. They were used just as the "hymns of praise" were, of which we read in the *Testamentum Domini*. And the occurrence of *Hallelujah* is so rare in Christian writings of the Eastern Church before the fifth century, and is so frequently associated with baptismal rejoicing as soon as the liturgical literature becomes abundant, that some support is thus given to the view of the Odes here taken, viz. that they were intended for use by catechumens or by the newly baptized.

Further, we have yet another notable rubric in the section of the *Testamentum Domini*, which treats of the offices for the Catechumens[3], viz. "In the forty days of Pascha, let the people abide in the temple, keeping vigil and praying, hearing the Scriptures and *hymns of praise* and the books of doctrine." If I am right in identifying the "hymns of praise" of the *Testamentum* with the ᾠδαί, which include the Odes of Solomon, we reach the important conclusion that it was customary to sing these latter during Lent. It is curious that the number of our *Odes* is exactly 42, which would be one for each day of Lent, beginning with the first Sunday in Lent and ending with Easter Eve. This was the period during which the Catechetical Lectures of Cyril of Jerusalem were delivered; there were some days on which there was no Lecture, but the first was given on the first Sunday, and the last on Easter Eve. The *Testamentum* is a composite book, and the dates of its several parts have not been

---

[1] See Cabrol, *l.c.*
[2] Cp. Denzinger, *l.c.* i. 207, 270, 286 and *passim*.
[3] II. 8.

exactly determined; but it presents to us, at any rate, the practice of the Asian (perhaps we might say "Syrian") Church during the earlier part of the fourth century, and thus it may be fairly compared with the information supplied by Cyril's lectures.

§ 11. *Cyril of Jerusalem.*

We now come on a curious coincidence. The *Procatechesis* of Cyril was delivered as an introduction to his course on the first Sunday in Lent (about the year 348). Let us place its opening phrases beside the first of our Odes:

CYRIL, *Procat.* 1[1].

Already there is an odour of blessedness upon you, O ye who are being enlightened; already ye are gathering the spiritual *blossoms* for the *weaving* of heavenly *crowns*; already the fragrance of the Holy Spirit has breathed upon you; already ye have gathered round the vestibule of the King's palace; may ye be led in also by the King! For there have now appeared *blossoms* on the trees; may the *fruit* also be *perfect*!

ODE 1.

The Lord is on my head like a *crown*, and I shall not be without Him. A *crown* of truth has been *woven* for me, and it has caused thy shoots to grow in me. For it is not like a withered *crown* which *blossometh* not; but thou livest upon my head, and thou hast *blossomed* upon my head. Thy *fruits* are full grown and *perfect*, full of thy salvation.

The words common to Cyril and the Odist have been italicised in the foregoing extracts, and it is remarkable how close is the agreement. The opening exhortation of Cyril, that is, speaks of the crowns of the baptized, not made of faded blossoms, but of those which being alive bear the promise of bringing forth fruit to perfection. This is exactly the thought of the Odist; and the question offers itself, Was this topic suggested to Cyril by the words of the hymn sung by the catechumens, as they assembled for instruction? Standing by itself, we could make little, perhaps, of the agreement between Ode i and the *Procatechesis* or Introductory Lecture; but when we notice that Ode xlii, the last of

[1] I append the Greek: ἤδη μακαριότητος ὀσμὴ πρὸς ὑμᾶς, ὦ φωτιζόμενοι· ἤδη τὰ νοητὰ ἄνθη συλλέγετε πρὸς πλοκὴν ἐπουρανίων στεφάνων· ἤδη τοῦ πνεύματος τοῦ ἁγίου ἔπνευσεν ἡ εὐωδία· ἤδη περὶ τὸ προαύλιον τῶν βασιλείων γεγόνατε· γένοιτο δὲ καὶ ὑπὸ τοῦ βασιλέως εἰσαχθῆτε· ἄνθη γὰρ νῦν ἐφάνη τῶν δένδρων· γένοιτο δὲ ἵνα καὶ ὁ καρπὸς τέλειος ᾖ.

the series, explicitly deals with the Preaching of Christ in Hades and His Conquest of Death, we naturally are reminded of the suitability of this topic to Easter Eve, when Ode xlii would be prescribed for recitation, if we are right in thinking that the "Odes of Solomon" were adapted for daily use during the forty-two days of Lent, when the candidates for baptism received instruction.

This inference, however, is probably too bold. What may be said with confidence is that the coincidence between the phrases of Cyril's *Procatechesis* and Ode i cannot be due to chance. If Cyril did not know Ode i, we should conclude that both his exhortations and Ode i contain reminiscences of phrases or ritual acts from the baptismal offices[1]. This in itself is noteworthy, and important for the interpretation of the Odes.

The passage which has been cited above[2] from the *Synopsis* of Pseudo-Athanasius shews that there was at one time a practice of reading non-canonical literature to the catechumens, and among these books outside the canon the Odes of Solomon are expressly named in the *Synopsis*. Cyril deprecates any such practice. "Read none of the apocryphal writings" is his counsel[3], which would have been an unnecessary prohibition had he not been conscious that there was a danger of the catechumens being misled by books which had not full canonical authority. It appears, however, from the similarities which have just been pointed out between Cyril's *Procatechesis* and Ode i, that he, at any rate, was familiar with that Ode, and that the catechumens to whom he spoke may have known it also.

§ 12. *Baptismal hymns in the early Church.*

That it was a custom in the early Church to receive the newly baptized with psalmody and singing is stated by Gregory Nazianzen[4]; and we possess among the works of Ephraim Syrus a collection of hymns sung on the Feast of Epiphany, which are placed in the mouths of those just admitted to baptism and express the joy of the Christian soul. They present many striking resemblances to

[1] See p. 21.   [2] p. 11.   [3] *Cat.* iv. 33.
[4] *Oratio*, xl. 46.

the Odes of Solomon, at once in their spiritual exaltation and in their mystical allusiveness. No. 13 of the series may fitly be cited here at length[1].

St Ephraim:

Hymn of the Baptized.

(*Resp.*—Brethren, sing praises, to the Son of the Lord of all; Who has bound for you crowns, such as kings long for!)

1. Your garments glisten, my brethren, as snow;—and fair is your shining in the likeness of Angels!
2. In the likeness of Angels, ye have come up, beloved,—from Jordan's river, in the armour of the Holy Ghost.
3. The bridal chamber that fails not, my brethren, ye have received;—and the glory of Adam's house to-day ye have put on.
4. The judgement that *came* of the fruit, was Adam's condemnation:—but for you victory, has arisen this day.
5. Your vesture is shining, and goodly your crowns:—which the Firstborn has bound for you, by the priests' hand this day.
6. Woe in Paradise, did Adam receive:—but you have received, glory this day.
7. The armour of victory, ye put on, my beloved:—in the hour when the priest, invoked the Holy Ghost.
8. The Angels rejoice, men here below exult:—in your feast, my brethren, wherein is no foulness.
9. The good things of Heaven, my brethren, ye have received:—beware of the Evil One, lest he despoil you.
10. The day when He dawned, the Heavenly King:—opens for you His door, and bids you enter Eden.
11. Crowns that fade not away, are set on your heads:—hymns of praise hourly, let your mouths sing.
12. Adam, by means of the fruit, *God* cast forth in sorrow:—but you He makes glad, in the bridechamber of joy.
13. Who would not rejoice, in your bridechamber, my brethren?—for the Father with His Son, and the Spirit rejoice in you.
14. Unto you shall the Father, be a wall of strength:—and the Son a Redeemer, and the Spirit a guard.
15. Martyrs by their blood, glorify their crowns:—but you our Redeemer, by His Blood glorifies.
16. Watchers and Angels, joy over the repentant:—they shall joy over you, my brethren, that unto them ye are made like.

---

[1] This translation is taken from Dr Gwynn's edition of Ephraim (*Nicene and Post Nicene Fathers*, vol. XIII. p. 283); it is due to Rev. A. E. Johnston.

17. The fruit which Adam, tasted not in Paradise:—this day in your mouths, has been placed with joy.

18. Our Redeemer figured, His Body by the tree:—whereof Adam tasted not, because he had sinned.

19. The Evil One made war, and subdued Adam's house:—through your baptism, my brethren lo! he is subdued this day.

20. Great is the victory, but to-day you have won:—if so be ye neglect not, you shall not perish, my brethren.

21. Glory to them that are robed, glory to Adam's house!—in the birth that *is* from the water, let them rejoice and be blessed.

22. Praise to Him Who has robed, His Churches in glory!—glory to Him Who has magnified, the race of Adam's house.

This hymn takes up thoughts which had already been expressed in the baptismal rite and puts them into verse, while baptism is not explicitly mentioned.

Another baptismal hymn, very like that of Ephraim, is found in the seventh century baptismal rite which bears the name of Severus, the Monophysite Patriarch of Antioch. Denzinger's Latin translation is as follows[1]:

1. Fratres canite gloriam Filio Domini universorum, qui coronam vobis nexuit, quam reges desiderarunt.

2. Illustrate vestimenta vestra et candidi estote, ut nix: et splendores vestri instar angelorum luceant.

3. Instar angelorum, ascendistis, carissimi, e Iordane fluvio per virtutem Spiritus Sancti.

4. Coronas haud marcescentes, fratres, accepistis: et gloriam Adae hodie induistis.

5. Fructus quem Adam in Paradiso non gustavit, hodie in oribus vestris positus est.

6. Bona caelestia, fratres, accepistis, cavete a malo ne vos diripiat.

It will be observed that *vv.* 1, 2, 3, 17 of Ephraim's hymn are very similar to *vv.* 2, 3, 4, 5 of the hymn from the Syriac baptismal office. Both recall (*a*) the white robes of the neophytes, (*b*) the crowning of the neophytes with garlands, and (*c*) the idea that the fruit of the tree of life, forbidden to Adam, is offered to the baptized Christian. We shall see, as we proceed, that similar reminiscences lie behind the language of the Odes; cp. Odes xxi 2, i 3, xi 14, and the notes on these passages.

[1] Denzinger, *Ritus Orientalium*, I. 315; cp. p. 288, and for a longer form p. 301.

Other hymns for Epiphany which bear comparison with those just cited, and also with our Odes, are the Hymns of Severus of Antioch[1], and the Hymns of Cosmas of Jerusalem[2]. Parallels from these to the Odes will be given in the notes, but the general character of the poems—especially those of Severus—recalls the Odes of Solomon quite as much as their similarity in details at special points. See *e.g.* the Hymn of Severus quoted in the note on Ode xi 10.

§ 13. *Topics not mentioned in the Odes.*

A feature in which our Odes remarkably resemble many of hese Epiphany hymns, of Ephraim, of Severus, and of Cosmas, is the untroubled joyousness which they express. From beginning to end of the Odes there is no mention of sin, of repentance, or of forgiveness; the "adversaries[3]" against whom the singer has to contend are often in his thoughts, and there is no doubt that here spiritual foes are in question, but he does not explicitly speak of sin. Exactly the same phenomena appear in the Epiphany hymns of Cosmas. It would seem that so convinced is the new Christian of the efficacy of baptism for the remission of sins that no place can be found in his song for thoughts of the perils of sin in the future. As Hermas has it: "He that hath received remission of sins ought no longer to sin, but to dwell in purity[4]."

Other omissions are noteworthy. The Name of Jesus does not once occur, although the Christology of the Odes is of a high order. But this may not be significant, for the same omission may be observed in the *Shepherd* of Hermas, undoubtedly a Christian composition.

Again, the Odist betrays complete familiarity, as we shall see, with the story of the Passion of Christ as recorded in the New Testament, and he knows some recondite passages of Old Testament prophecy[5]. But he never quotes directly, either from the Old Testament or the New[6].

He never mentions Baptism, although (in the view which is here expounded) he alludes again and again to baptismal doctrine

---

[1] *Patr. Orient.* vi. 1.   [2] Migne, *P.G.* xcviii. col. 459 ff.
[3] See § 21 below.   [4] *Mand.* iv. 3.   [5] See Odes vi 7, xvii 8.
[6] See § 16 below.

and to the baptismal rite; and he does not once hint at the Eucharist, neither mentioning it directly, nor making indirect reference to its virtue[1].

Burkitt[2] explains these omissions by the assumed Solomonic authorship of the Odes. Pseudepigraphical literature had its rules, and these would forbid so glaring an anachronism as the explicit statement of Christian doctrine in a work by "Solomon." The observation is important and interesting; but it would be quite in character for "Solomon" to quote and use the Old Testament much more freely than our Odist does. The "Psalms of Solomon" are almost a *cento* from the Hebrew Scriptures.

§ 14. *The Disciplina Arcani.*

A more probable explanation of these omissions is provided by the *disciplina arcani* of the Church in the early centuries. Christianity was not indeed a secret cult, like some of the pagan religions. But so soon as the catechumenate became an established institution, towards the end of the second century, it was the rule of the Church's teachers to give full instruction in the Church's mysteries only to the baptized. This may have been, as Batiffol has argued[3], little more than a convention, and it was probably always possible for a pagan scholar like Celsus to find out all that he desired to know about Christian doctrine. But it was a well recognised convention of the Church's teachers that the teaching was to be gradual, beginning with the instruction of Catechumens in the first principles of the Faith, and culminating in the explanation of the Christian mysteries, especially of the Eucharist, to those who had received baptism. This may be seen clearly by an inspection of Cyril's Catechetical Lectures, which were followed by the five *Mystagogica* delivered after the baptism of the Catechumens had taken place. Cyril speaks strongly of the *disciplina arcani* which he expected even the catechumens to observe: "If a Catechumen ask thee what the teachers have said, tell nothing to him that is without. For we deliver to thee a

---

[1] See, however, on Ode xx 1.
[2] *Journ. of Theol. Studies*, April, 1912.
[3] See his essay *L'Arcane* in *Études d'Histoire et de Théologie Positive* (1902).

mystery, and a hope of the life to come. Guard the mystery for Him who gives the reward....Thou art now standing on the border; take heed, pray, to tell nothing out; not that the things spoken are not worthy to be told, but because his ear is unworthy to receive. Thou wast once thyself a Catechumen, and I described not what lay before thee. When by experience thou hast learned how high are the matters of our teaching, then thou wilt know that the Catechumens are not worthy to hear them[1]." And again: "These mysteries which the Church now explains to thee who art passing out of the class of Catechumens, it is not the custom to explain to heathen. For to a heathen we do not explain the mysteries concerning Father, Son, and Holy Ghost, nor before Catechumens do we speak plainly of the mysteries; but many things we often speak in a veiled way, that the believers who know may understand, and they who know not may get no hurt[2]." In this last sentence is contained, as I would urge, the key to the cryptic phraseology of the Odes of Solomon. They were intended for public worship, but are so expressed that they do not reveal explicitly any of the principles of the Faith.

Basil speaks in the same spirit as Cyril of the *disciplina arcani*, and even more emphatically. The customs, he says, of the baptismal ritual are not written down, but they "come from that unpublished and secret teaching which our fathers guarded in a silence out of the reach of curious meddling and inquisitive investigations....What the uninitiated are not even allowed to look at was hardly likely to be paraded publicly in written documents[3]."

The preparation of candidates for baptism was definitely organised by the end of the second century. We have in the *Didache* the outlines of such moral instruction as was given; and Justin Martyr[4] seems to refer to a course of preparatory instruction. It is set forth more fully in Book vii of the Apostolical Constitutions and in Cyril's Catechetical Lectures. Including, at any rate, the doctrine of the Trinity, of Creation and of Providence, the rewards of the righteous and the punishment of the wicked, it came at last (as in Cyril) to follow the order of the Creed. But

---
[1] *Procat.* 12.   [2] *Cat.* vi. 29.   [3] *De Spir. Sancto*, 27.
[4] *Apol.* i. 61.

no instruction on the Eucharist was given until after baptism, and this enables us to understand the absence of allusions to that Sacrament in the Odes. This would be difficult to explain if the Odes are regarded as ordinary Christian hymns, for the use of the faithful, but it is quite harmonious with the view that they were associated rather with the teaching of the Catechumens.

Edessa, Antioch, and Caesarea, as great centres of Christian life, had doubtless a fully organised system of catechetical instruction, such as we know of at Alexandria; and of this we have, as it seems, an early trace in the *Odes of Solomon*.

§ 15. *Christian doctrine in the Odes.*

It is desirable, at this point, to examine which of the Articles of the Creed are implicit in the Odes. Certainly, they presuppose the doctrine of the Trinity. "The Son is the cup, and He who was milked is the Father, and the Holy Spirit milked Him" (xix 2) is sufficient to establish this, even if we had not "The Name of the Father was on it, and of the Son, and of the Holy Spirit, to rule for ever and ever" (xxiii 20).

The doctrine of God the Father as Creator naturally appears. "Thou, O God, hast made all things" (iv 14); "He hath given a mouth to His creation" (vii 28); "Be enriched in God the Father" (ix 4) are specimen passages. It will be noticed that the last cited in its explicit mention of God the *Father* presupposes a further belief in God the *Son*.

The Son of God is the Messiah, the Christ: "The Son of the Most High appeared in the perfection of His Father, and light dawned from the Word that was beforetime in Him; the Messiah is truly one, and He was known before the foundation of the world" (xli 14 f.). He is "the Lord Messiah" (xvii 14), or "our Lord Messiah" (xxxix 10), and "the Lord's Messiah" (xxix 6; cp. Luke ii 26). "Life we receive in His Messiah" (xli 3). He was born of a Virgin (xix 6 f.), and became incarnate: "He became like me, in order that I might receive Him: He was reckoned like myself in order that I might put Him on" (vii 5, 6). He was crucified; for Ode xlii 2 speaks of "the outspread tree which was set up on the way of the Righteous One" (cp. xxvii

3), and the gall and vinegar of the Passion are alluded to in xlii. 17. The purpose of His humiliation was "that I might redeem my people" (xxxi 10), and "to lead captive a good captivity for freedom" (x 3). He is "the Saviour who makes alive and does not reject our souls" (xli 12). "The Descent into Hell" was not a formulated article of the Creed, either in East or West, when our Odes were written; but a fully developed belief in Christ's Visitation of Hades was current at a very early date, and the Odes allude to this several times (see xvii 9—11 and especially Ode xlii 15 f.). This belief in the Harrowing of Hell virtually implies the Resurrection of Christ: He is "the Man who was humbled and exalted by His own righteousness" (xli 13); cp. "I rose up and am with them" (xlii 6).

Belief in the Holy Spirit is behind all the thoughts of the Odist (cp. xi 2, xiv 8, xxviii 2, xxxvi 1 and see xix 2, xxiii 20 for explicitly Christian expressions). We have also assertions of the immortality of the believer (ix 3, iii 10); but we have nothing as to the Resurrection of the Body, which, as we learn from the *Testamentum Domini*[1], was not explained to catechumens before baptism.

§ 16. *Allusions to Holy Scripture.*

There is no explicit quotation either from the Old Testament or the New Testament in the Odes, although there are many allusions both to the Jewish and the Christian Scriptures. Some of the more interesting are here tabulated, but the list is not exhaustive.

Exod. xxii 26, 27. Cp.: "Neither shalt thou seek to deceive thy neighbour, neither shalt thou deprive him of the covering of his nakedness" (Ode xx 5).

Josh. iii 15, 17; iv 9. Cp.: "His footprints stand firm on the water...they are as firm as a (piece of) wood that is truly set up. And the waves are lifted up on this side and on that, but the footsteps of our Lord Christ stand firm, and are not obliterated" (Ode xxxix 8).

Ps. xix 2, 4. Cp.: "The treasure chamber of the light is the sun, and the treasury of the darkness is the night...and their

---

[1] II. 10.

alternations one to the other speak the beauty of God" (Ode xvi 16).

Ps. xxii 16. Cp.: "They came round me like mad dogs who ignorantly attack their masters" (Ode xxviii 11).

Ps. xlviii 14. Cp.: "Be my guide even unto the end" (Ode xiv 4).

Ps. lxxi 1. Cp.: "The Lord is my hope; in Him I shall not be confounded" (Ode xxix 1).

Ps. c 3. Cp.: "that they may recognise Him that made them; and that they might not suppose that they came of themselves" (Ode vii 15).

Ps. cxxiii 2. Cp.: "As the eyes of a son to his father, so are my eyes, O Lord, at all times towards thee" (Ode xiv 1).

Prov. viii 22(?) Cp.: "He who possessed me from the beginning" (Ode xli 9).

Isa. xlv 2, 3 (see also Ps. cvii 16). Cp.: "I opened the doors that were closed and brake in pieces the bars of iron" (Ode xvii 8).

Isa. lii 14(?). Cp.: "All those will be astonished that see me" (Ode xli 8).

Ezek. xxxvii 1 f. Cp.: "Thou didst take dead bones and didst cover them with bodies; they were motionless and thou didst give them energy for life" (Ode xxii 9).

Ezek. xlvii 1 f. Cp.: "There went forth a stream and became a river great and broad, for it flooded and broke up everything and it brought to the temple" (Ode vi 7).

St Matt. iii 16. Cp.: "The Dove fluttered over the Christ" (Ode xxiv 1).

St Matt. xvi 18. Cp.: "That the foundation of everything might be thy Rock, and on it thou didst build thy kingdom" (Ode xxii 12).

St Matt. xxviii 19. Cp.: "A great tablet which was wholly written by the finger of God, and the name of the Father was on it, and of the Son, and of the Holy Spirit" (Ode xxiii 19).

St Luke i 51, 52. Cp.: "That I might subdue the imaginations of the peoples; and the power of the men of might to bring them low" (Ode xxix 8).

St Luke i 69—73. Cp.: "That I might redeem my people

and inherit it, and that I might not make void my promises to the fathers, to whom I promised the salvation of their seed" (Ode xxxi 11).

St John i 3. Cp.: "The worlds were made by His word" (Ode xvi 20).

St John xvii 6, 11. Cp.: "He offered to Him the sons that were in His hands. And His face was justified, for thus His holy Father had given to Him" (Ode xxxi 4, 5).

Rom. xi 29. Cp.: "There is no repentance with thee, that thou shouldest repent of anything that thou hast promised" (Ode iv 11).

Gal. iii 27. Cp.: "He was reckoned like myself in order that I might put Him on" (Ode vii 6; see also Ode xiii 2, xxxiii 10).

Hebr. i 2. Cp.: "He inherited...everything" (Ode xxiii 17).

Hebr. iv 12. Cp.: "The swiftness of the Word cannot be expressed, and according to its swiftness so is its sharpness" (Ode xii 5).

1 Pet. i 20. Cp.: "He was known before the foundation of the world" (Ode xli 16).

1 John iv 19. Cp.: "I should not have known how to love the Lord, if He had not loved me" (Ode iii 3).

There seems no sure trace of the Apocalypse, although there are passages which might be thought to carry allusions to that book (see on Odes iii 11, ix 12 and xxxviii 10 f.). The Apocalypse was little known in Syria in the early centuries. Ephraim seems to have known it, indeed, and perhaps Aphrahat; but it was not current in a Syriac version until after their time[1].

§ 17. *The Odes not Gnostic.*

Of Gnosticism there is no sure trace in the Odes. The passage which most strongly suggests Gnostic speculation is in Ode xii. Here we have the Word described as Light and the Dawning of Thought (ἔννοια). By it the worlds (or Aeons) talk to each other: "in the Word there were those that were silent, and from it came Love and Concord." Finally, "the dwelling place of the Word is Man, and its Truth is Love." The phraseology recalls the

---

[1] See Gwynn, *The Apocalypse of St John in Syriac*, pp. c—ciii.

Valentinian doctrine of the emanation of the *Aeons* as set forth by Irenaeus[1], who explains that the Valentinians held the starting-point of the evolution to be the union of Bythos and *Ennoia*, another name for which is *Silence*. This issues in Nous and *Aletheia*: which again give rise to *Logos* and Zoe, the parents of *Anthropos* and Ecclesia. Among the Aeons which proceed from the last combination is *Agape*. The italicised terms occur also in Ode xii in close juxtaposition, but none of them is really distinctive of Gnosticism in contrast with an orthodox Christian philosophy, such as that of the Fourth Gospel. The conception of the Word as containing within itself "those that were silent" is different from that of the Word issuing forth from Silence which is found in Ignatius (*ad Magnes.* 8) as well as in the Gnostic systems; and a close parallel to the language of our Odist may be adduced from a writer so entirely orthodox as Augustine. "*Verbum* eius ipse Christus, *in quo requiescunt angeli* et omnes caelestes mundissimi spiritus *in sancto silentio*[2]." Again, the identification of the Word with the Thought ($\check{\epsilon}\nu\nu o\iota a$) of God, which appears several times again in the Odes (xvi 20, xxviii 18, xli 10, 11, ix 2, and cp. xxiii 5) is explicit in Irenaeus: "*Cogitatio enim eius Logos et Logos mens, et omnia concludens mens ipse Pater*[3]." We may compare also the prayer in the Morning Office of the *Testamentum Domini*, where our Lord is addressed as "*the Thought of the Father*, who didst found the worlds in prudence and wisdom[4]"; and again in a Hymn of Praise to the Father, in c. xxxii of the same work, we have "We praise thee, O Lord, Who didst send *thy Thought*, thy Word, thy Wisdom, thy Energy, Him who is of old and was with thee before the worlds." There is, therefore, no necessity to treat the "silent ones" (xii 8) and the "Thought of the Most High" (xxviii 18) of our Odes as betraying any leaning to the Gnostic speculations about Sigé and Ennoia.

The perversion of the Odes to Gnostic uses in the *Pistis Sophia* does not prove them Gnostic any more than the perversion of the Fourth Gospel by the Valentinians proves it to have been composed with a Valentinian tendency[5].

[1] *Adv. Haer.* I. 1 ff.
[2] *De Cat. Rud.* 17 (28).
[3] *Adv. Haer.* II. 28. 5.
[4] I. xxvi.
[5] See Fries, *Zeitschr. für die N.T. Wiss.* 1911, pp. 108 ff.

There is one passage (Ode xxxii 2) in which the Christology of the Odes seems to contain elements which point to a period when the Church had begun to formulate its doctrine in set phrases (see note *in loc.*). But I am unable to find, as Mgr. Batiffol does[1], anything in the doctrine of the Person of Christ, as set forth by our Odist, which savours of Docetism.

§ 18. *The Logos Doctrine in the Odes.*

The doctrine of the Word in the Odes is very explicit. The Word, as we have seen[2], is the Thought of God; and this Thought is Life (ix 3) and Light (xii 7). "Light dawned from the Word that was beforetime in Him" (xli 15): so that the *pre-existence* of the Word is recognised, as again "He was before anything came into being" (xvi 19). This seems to be the meaning also of the phrases at the end of Ode xxviii, where the singer is speaking *ex ore Christi*: "They sought to bring to nought the memory of Him who was before them, for nothing is prior to the thought of the Most High." Harnack will not allow that *v.* 15 of the same Ode is spoken in reference to Christ; but the words seem to recall John viii 58 and the great pronouncement "Before Abraham was I am," which led the Jews to cast stones at Him. "They sought for my death and did not find it; for I was older than their recollection; and vainly did they make attack upon me...they sought to destroy the memory of Him who was before them." The remarkable expression "The Truth, who was self-originate" (xxxii 2) as applied to Christ, should also be noticed.

The Word is the agent of creation, for "the worlds were made by His Word and by the Thought of His heart" (xvi 20). It is the medium of the intercommunication of created things. "By it the worlds talk one to the other" (xii 8); with which should be compared the passage (clearly reminiscent of Ps. xix 2, 4) at the end of Ode xvi: "The treasure chamber of the light is the sun, and the treasury of the darkness is the night; and He made the sun for the day that it may be bright, but night brings darkness over the face of the land; and their alternations one to the other

---

[1] *Les Odes de Salomon*, pp. 94 ff. [2] *Supra*, p. 29.

speak the beauty of God: and there is nothing that is without the Lord."

The Johannine statements of the Pre-existence of the Word with God, and of the creation of all things by Him (John i 2, 3) are thus expanded and emphasised. The language of Hebr. i 2 is also suggested to us; and other passages in the same Odes (xii and xvi) recall Hebr. iv 12. "The Word of the Lord searches out all things" (xvi 9). "The swiftness of the Word cannot be expressed, and according to its swiftness so is its sharpness: and its course knows no limit. Never doth it fail, but it stands sure; and it knows not descent, nor the way of it" (xii 5, 6).

Finally, the Incarnation of the Word is explicitly stated: "the dwelling place of the Word is man" (xii 11, cp. Ode xxii 12), and hence we reach the thought of the continual abiding of God with man, "His Word is with us in all our way" (xli 11)[1].

The explicitness of this teaching as to the Word is noteworthy, when we remember that the Odes are, as it seems, of Palestinian or Syrian origin, and not later than 180 A.D. They exhibit the tendencies of Judaeo-Christian piety at that time and in that region; and they shew how truly Palestinian the Logos doctrine is. There is nothing of Philo or the Alexandrian philosophy in their doctrine of the Word. The writer seems, indeed, to have known the Johannine writings, although he does not directly quote them; but the doctrine of Christ as the Logos, of which he sings in joy and exultation, is not dependent on a few phrases in the Prologue to the Fourth Gospel; it is deep-rooted in his thought. The Odes, in short, provide us with a welcome illustration of that mystical side of Christian teaching which has been generally traced to Hellenic rather than to Hebrew influences. They shew how congenial to Palestine as well as to Greece was this lofty conception of Christ, as the Word, the Light, the Life.

---

[1] There is an interesting reference to Odes in Eusebius (*H.E.* v. 28) in an extract which is probably from Hippolytus: "How many Psalms and Odes written by the faithful brethren from the beginning hymn Christ as the Word of God, speaking of Him as Divine!" This would serve well as a description of such Odes as nos. 7, 12, 15, 16, of our collection.

§ 19. *The Baptism of Christ and the Descent into Hades.*

The connexion in early Christian thought between the Baptism of Christ and His Descent into Hades is curious and remarkable. Its starting-point is the word ἄβυσσος. In the Old Testament this stands for "the deep[1]," the underlying waters by which the earth was covered at the first (Gen. i 2), but on which it afterwards rested (Ps. xxiv 2, cxxxvi 6), and from which its springs and rivers welled up (cp. Gen. vii 11). It is thus the "underworld," the region below land and sea alike, with which all waters, of rivers or ocean, are in communication. This underworld was regarded in New Testament times as the abode of demons (Luke viii 31, Rev. ix 1, xi 7, xvii 8, xx 1), an idea expressed clearly by Origen in his comment on Gen. i 2[2]: "Quae est abyssus? Illa nimirum, in qua erit diabolus et angeli eius," referring to Luke viii 31; and again: "separatus ab ea aqua, quae subtus est, id est, aqua abyssi, in qua tenebrae sunt dicuntur, in qua princeps huius mundi, et adversarius draco, et angeli eius habitant." It was to this "abyss" that, according to St Paul (Rom. x 7), Christ descended after His Passion.

In the beginning of things darkness was upon the abyss, and the Spirit brooded upon (for that is the force of the Hebrew) the waters. Then the darkness was dispelled by the Divine Word "Let there be light." Later on, the waters were "gathered together into one place," and the dry land appeared (Gen. i 9). It is thus described in Job xxxviii 8:

> ἔφραξα δὲ θάλασσαν πύλαις...
> ....
> ἐθέμην δὲ αὐτῇ ὅρια,
> περιθεὶς κλεῖθρα καὶ πύλας,

and in Ps. xxxii (xxxiii) 7:

> συνάγων ὡς ἀσκὸν ὕδατα θαλάσσης
> τιθεὶς ἐν θησαυροῖς ἀβύσσους.

Now this Epiphany of the Spirit upon the primeval waters was supposed to have its counterpart in the Baptism of our Lord.

---

[1] See Hastings' *Dict. of the Bible, s.v.* "Abyss."
[2] *Sel. in Genesin* (Lommatzsch, VIII. 106).

As of old, the Spirit brooded upon the waters of Jordan, for thus it is expressed in the baptismal *Ordo* of Severus of Antioch: "Spiritus sanctus in similitudinem columbae *volans*[1] descendit, mansitque super caput filii et *super aquas incubavit*[2]." Moses bar Kepha explicitly makes this comparison in his Exposition of Baptism: "As the Spirit of God brooded upon the waters in the beginning of creation that it might impart to them generative and fertilising power, so also here the Holy Spirit broods upon the waters of baptism through the pouring out of the *myron* [oil] upon them[3]." So, too, a bright light (it was said) appeared from heaven[4], after the Divine Voice "This is my beloved Son."

And that the coercing of the waters of old was not absent from the thought of the compilers of the baptismal *ordines* is apparent from such invocations as these: "...qui in unam molem aquam coarctas, qui claudis abyssum[5]"; or again, "...qui in unum locum aquas congregasti ac mare coercuisti *abyssosque obserasti*, easque sancto et gloriosissimo nomine tuo *obsignasti*...tu confregisti capita draconis super aquas[6]."

So also we find in an Armenian baptismal rite the words: "By thy dread command, thou didst *close up the abysses and make them fast*...thou didst bruise the head of the dragon upon the waters[7]."

Next, it is to be observed that all the baptismal rituals bring in the idea that the waters were terrified at the coming of Christ for baptism. They quote[8] Ps. lxxvi (lxxvii) 17, εἴδοσάν σε ὕδατα καὶ ἐφοβήθησαν καὶ ἐταράχθησαν ἄβυσσοι, or Ps. cxiii (cxiv) 3, ἡ θάλασσα εἶδεν καὶ ἔφυγεν, ὁ Ἰορδάνης ἐστράφη εἰς τὰ ὀπίσω, or

---

[1] Cp. Ode xxiv 1.   [2] Denzinger, *Rit. Orient.* I. 311.

[3] § 13 quoted by Aytoun, *Expositor*, Oct. 1911, p. 351. Cp. Denzinger, *l.c.* I. 345.

[4] So Epiphanius (*Haer.* xxx. 13); Justin, *Tryph.* 88; and cp. *Orac. Sibyll.* VII. 83.

[5] Assemani, *Cod. Lit.* II. 146.

[6] Assemani, *Cod. Lit.* II. 170, from a Coptic office (Denzinger, *l.c.* I. 205). Cp. Ode xxiv 5.

[7] Conybeare, *Rituale Armenorum*, p. 101. Cp. Denzinger, *l.c.* I. 394.

[8] It is hardly necessary to give references. The *Ordo* of Severus quotes all three passages. The first is quoted in Assemani's *Ordo Alexandr. Copt. et Aethiop.*; the second in the Mass of the Catechumens in the Liturgy of St Chrysostom; the third in the modern form of Blessing the Waters, and in the modern Nestorian rite. Cp. Denzinger, *l.c.* I. 207, 219, 227, 228, 282, 313, etc.

Ps. xxviii (xxix) 3, φωνὴ κυρίου ἐπὶ τῶν ὑδάτων, as forecasting the terrors inspired by the Coming of the Christ to the Jordan. This idea is not peculiar to the rituals, ancient or modern. It is also found in Christian art. In more than one representation of the Baptism of Christ, Jordan is depicted allegorically in the water below as starting away in astonished fear[1]. The idea appears in Hippolytus[2], and in Origen who paraphrases Ps. lxxvi (lxxvii) 17, αἱ ἄβυσσοι τὰς καταχθονίους δυνάμεις δηλοῦσιν, αἵτινες ἐν τῇ παρουσίᾳ Χριστοῦ ἐταράχθησαν.

This last quotation introduces a new point, viz. that not only were the waters afraid, but the demons and evil spirits were scared away. Thus there is a prayer in the baptismal *Ordo* of Severus of Antioch[3]: "...fugiant itaque umbrae invisibiles et aëriae, quaeso te, domine, neque delitescat in aquis istis tenebrosus daemon."

We have passed from the Baptism of Christ to the baptism of Christians, and we are next to notice that baptism, in early Christian thought, was a release from bondage. Thus Barnabas (§ 11) quotes as predictive of baptism the words of Isaiah xlv 2, 3, "I will go before thee and level mountains and crush gates of brass and break in pieces bolts of iron, and I will give thee treasures, dark, concealed, unseen, that they may know that I am the Lord God." Isaiah's words are themselves reminiscent of Ps. cvii 14, 16: "He brought them out of darkness and the shadow of death and brake their bonds in sunder....For he hath broken the gates of brass and cut the bars of iron in sunder."

The bondage from which we are released is, of course, the bondage of sin; and the cognate thought that in baptism we are restored to Paradise, to that state from which Adam fell, the guilt of sin being annulled, is common in the Fathers. Thus Origen's comment on ἔθετο αὐτὸν ἐν τῷ παραδείσῳ (Gen. ii 8) is: οἱ ἀναγεννώμενοι διὰ τοῦ θείου βαπτίσματος ἐν τῷ παραδείσῳ τίθενται, τουτέστιν, ἐν τῇ ἐκκλησίᾳ ἐργάζεσθαι τὰ ἔνδον ὄντα ἔργα πνευματικά. So Gregory of Nyssa, in his Sermon on Christ's Baptism, exclaims: "The Jordan is glorified by regenerating men,

---

[1] See C. F. Rogers, "Baptism and Christian Archaeology" in *Studia Bibl. et Eccl.* v. 4, pp. 290, 291.

[2] *De Theoph.* 2. Cp. also Ephraim, *Epiphany Hymns*, xiv. 31, and Ode xxiv 2, 3.

[3] Denzinger, *l.c.* i. p. 306; cp. also p. 275, and Assemani, *l.c.* ii. 226.

and planting them in the Paradise of God; and of them, as the words of the Psalmist say, ever blooming and bearing the foliage of virtues 'The leaf shall not wither' and God shall be glad receiving their fruit in due season[1]." In like manner, Paradise is described as the place of habitation of the baptized by Basil[2], who asks: σὺ δὲ πῶς ἐπανέλθῃς εἰς τὸν παράδεισον, μὴ σφραγισθεὶς τῷ βαπτίσματι; Once more, in the 13th of Ephraim's *Epiphany Hymns* we have: "He opens for you His door, and bids you enter Eden (ver. 10)...the fruit which Adam tasted not in Paradise, this day in your mouths has been placed (ver. 17)."

Thus, then, to summarise what has been collected of early Christian ideas about baptism: In baptism the powers of the underworld are terrified by the Advent of Christ, who breaks the brazen bars and releases His captives, bringing them back to the Paradise of man in his innocence. In baptism we are "buried with Him" (Rom. vi 4); we reproduce, as it were, on a lower plane, His experiences, having "become united with Him by the likeness of His death." We go down into the baptismal waters, that we may rise up with Him.

Now let us turn to the *gnosis* of the Descent into Hades and the "Harrowing of Hell" (cp. Eph. iv 9), so common in early and mediaeval Christian literature. The apocryphal *Descensus ad inferos* (probably a second century production) tells (ii 18) that John the Baptist announced to the patriarchs in Hades that he had baptized the Christ, adding that He would soon visit those who were in darkness and the shadow of death. Dr Harris quotes[3] the following passage: "Ego Johannes vocem patris de caelo super eum intonantem audivi et proclamantem, Hic est filius meus dilectus, in quo mihi bene complacuit. Ego ab eo responsum accepi quia ipse descensurus ad inferos." The idea occurs also in Origen, and more than once. He says of John Baptist, εἰς ᾅδου κατεβέβηκε προκηρύσσων τὸν κύριον, ἵνα προείπῃ αὐτὸν κατελευσόμενον[4]; and again in a passage of which only the Latin is extant, "Et mortuus est ante eum, ut ad inferna

---
[1] Cp. Cyril, *Hier. Cat.* i. 4: καταφυτεύῃ λοιπὸν εἰς τὸν νοητὸν παράδεισον.
[2] *Hom.* xiii. 2.
[3] p. 125 (ed. 2).
[4] *Hom.* ii. *in* 1 *Sam.* (Lommatzsch xi. 327).

descendens illius praedicaret adventum[1]." So in a Homily for Easter Eve, wrongly ascribed to Epiphanius, John Baptist is described as ὁ διττὸς πρόδρομος, καὶ κῆρυξ ζώντων καὶ νεκρῶν[2].

It would appear that the fancy was that the Descent of Christ into the waters of Jordan was quickly communicated to the dwellers in the abyss, and that it inspired them with terror. John Baptist brought the news and announced that Christ was coming down into the abyss itself. The tidings were preceded by the shining of a great light.

We have already seen that the Descent into Hades is alluded to by St Paul as a going down into the "abyss" (Rom. x 6); and a passage from the Old Testament which was quoted[3] as prefiguring the same event is Jonah ii 6, 7:

ἄβυσσος ἐκύκλωσέν με ἐσχάτη,
ἔδυ ἡ κεφαλή μου εἰς σχισμὰς ὀρέων,
κατέβην εἰς γῆν ἧς οἱ μοχλοὶ αὐτῆς κάτοχοι αἰώνιοι.

The purpose of the Descent is the redemption of mankind. As Cyril says[4]: κατῆλθεν εἰς τὰ καταχθόνια, ἵνα κἀκεῖθεν λυτρώσηται τοὺς δικαίους. The keepers of the gates of Hades are scared, an idea connected with the LXX. of Job xxxviii 17:

ἀνοίγονται δέ σοι φόβῳ πύλαι θανάτου·
πυλωροὶ δὲ ᾅδου ἰδόντες σε ἔπτηξαν;

The *Descensus ad inferos* proceeds[5]: "Et ecce subito infernus contremuit, et portae mortis et serae comminutae et vectes ferrei confracti sunt et ceciderunt in terram, et patefacta sunt omnia," *i.e.* the brazen gates and iron bars are broken, a reminiscence of Ps. cvii 16 and Isa. xlv 2, which, it will be noted, also occurs in connexion with the *gnosis* of Christ's baptism. Then the saints arise and come forth from Hades with Christ (cp. Matt. xxvii 52, 53), and are led into Paradise[6].

---
[1] *Hom.* IV. *in Lucam* (Lommatzsch v. 99).
[2] Migne, *P.G.* XLIII. 453.   [3] *e.g.* by Cyril, *Cat.* XIV. 20.
[4] *Cat.* IV. 11.   [5] *B.* VIII. (24).
[6] *Descensus* A. IX. (25). Bigg (on 1 Pet. iii 19) quotes, after Weber, two passages from the *Bereschit Rabba*: "But when they that are bound, they that are in Gehinnom, saw the light of the Messiah, they rejoiced to receive Him"; and, "This

We need not pursue further the fanciful details of the "Harrowing of Hell": enough has been said to shew that the same kind of language was used about the effects of Christ's Baptism (and also of the baptism of believers) that was used about the effects of His Descent to Hades. The going down into the abyss, the terror of evil spirits, the release of captives, their admission to Paradise—are ideas common to both[1]; and, as was said above, the starting-point of such speculations is the conception of the "abyss," the mysterious underworld with which communication is by water. Quite a large section of the Prayer of Initiation of catechumens in the *Testamentum Domini*[2] is occupied with a recital of Christ's victory in Hades.

Indeed, the connexion between the doctrine of baptism and the Victory of Christ in Hades is behind the custom of baptizing catechumens on Easter Eve.

These two beliefs, of the Ministry of Christ in Hades, and of the Efficacy of Baptism, are associated, it need hardly be said, in the well-known passage, 1 Pet. iii 19—21:

Ἐν ᾧ καὶ τοῖς ἐν φυλακῇ πνεύμασιν πορευθεὶς ἐκήρυξεν, ἀπειθήσασίν ποτε ὅτε ἀπεξεδέχετο ἡ τοῦ θεοῦ μακροθυμία ἐν ἡμέραις Νῶε κατασκευαζομένης κιβωτοῦ εἰς ἣν ὀλίγοι, τοῦτ' ἔστιν ὀκτὼ ψυχαί, διεσώθησαν δι' ὕδατος. ὃ [al. ᾧ] καὶ ὑμᾶς ἀντίτυπον νῦν σώζει βάπτισμα κ.τ.λ.

Here the baptismal waters are treated as the antitype of the waters of the Flood, suggested by the mention of Noah, as one of the patriarchs in Hades to whom Christ preached. No closer connexion is indicated, nor are there here any fanciful details of the Harrowing of Hell. Nevertheless, the juxtaposition of the two topics is noteworthy; and in more than one comment of the Fathers the connexion is between them represented as significant. Thus in Hermas[3] the idea is plainly expressed: ἔλαβον οὖν καὶ οὗτοι οἱ κεκοιμημένοι τὴν σφραγῖδα τοῦ υἱοῦ τοῦ θεοῦ καὶ εἰσῆλθον

is that which stands written: We shall rejoice and exult in Thee. When? When the captives climb up out of hell and the Shechinah at their head." These are Jewish sayings, and I do not know their date. But probably they betray the influence of Christian gnosis.

[1] Another point of contact is the comparison in the *Descensus ad inferos*, of the "oil from the tree of mercy" which Adam desired, with the baptismal chrism.
[2] I. 28. [3] *Sim.* IX. 16.

εἰς τὴν βασιλείαν τοῦ θεοῦ· πρὶν γάρ, φησί, φορέσαι τὸν ἄνθρωπον τὸ ὄνομα [τοῦ υἱοῦ] τοῦ θεοῦ, νεκρός ἐστιν· ὅταν δὲ λάβῃ τὴν σφραγῖδα, ἀποτίθεται τὴν νέκρωσιν καὶ ἀναλαμβάνει τὴν ζωήν. ἡ σφραγὶς οὖν τὸ ὕδωρ ἐστιν· εἰς τὸ ὕδωρ οὖν καταβαίνουσι νεκροί, καὶ ἀναβαίνουσι ζῶντες. κἀκείνοις οὖν ἐκηρύχθη ἡ σφραγὶς αὕτη, καὶ ἐχρήσατο αὐτῇ, ἵνα εἰσέλθωσιν εἰς τὴν βασιλείαν τοῦ θεοῦ...κατέβησαν οὖν μετ' αὐτῶν εἰς τὸ ὕδωρ, καὶ πάλιν ἀνέβησαν. ἀλλ' οὗτοι ζῶντες κατέβησαν [καὶ πάλιν ζῶντες ἀνέβησαν]· ἐκεῖνοι δὲ οἱ προκεκοιμημένοι νεκροὶ κατέβησαν, ζῶντες δὲ ἀνέβησαν.

The same thing appears in Irenaeus[1]: "Primogenitus enim mortuorum natus dominus, et in sinum suum recipiens pristinos patres, *regeneravit eos in vitam dei*...hic illos in evangelium vitae regeneravit," where the idea of *regeneration* as applied to the patriarchs is remarkable.

Again, Basil[2] explicitly speaks of our baptism as a reflection or imitation of Christ's Descent to Hades: πῶς οὖν κατορθοῦμεν τὴν εἰς ᾅδου κάθοδον, μιμούμενοι τὴν ταφὴν τοῦ Χριστοῦ διὰ τοῦ βαπτίσματος;

A Western testimony to the same comparison is provided by a declaration of the Fourth Council of Toledo[3] (633 A.D.): "Et ne forte cuiquam sit dubium huius simpli mysterium sacramenti, videat in eo mortem et resurrectionem Christi significari. Nam *in aquis mersio, quasi in infernum descensio est*; et rursus ab aquis emersio resurrectio est."

This idea is expanded in a Homily for Easter Eve[4], printed among the works of Epiphanius (although it is not his), from which some remarkable sentences must now be quoted. The writer first says of Easter Eve that this is the day on which is salvation τοῖς ἐπὶ τῆς γῆς καὶ τοῖς ἀπ' αἰῶνος ὑποκάτω τῆς γῆς, to those on earth and to those under the earth; by which words he refers to the baptism of catechumens and to the Preaching of Christ in Hades. He goes on to speak of a twofold life, διττὴν γέννησιν ὁμοῦ καὶ ἀναγέννησιν...νυκτὶ Χριστὸς ἐν Βηθλεὲμ γεννᾶται· νυκτὶ πάλιν ἐν τῇ Σιὼν ἀναγεννᾶται. But it will be

---
[1] *Adv. Haer.* III. 22. 4.
[2] *De spiritu sancto*, xv. 35.   [3] cap. 6.
[4] Pseudo-Epiphanius, *Hom.* II. *in Sabbato magno* (Migne, *P.G.* XLIII. col. 440 f.).

asked, how does the Birth of Christ at Bethlehem come into question here? The answer is curious. The Homilist urges that just as Christ passed through the unopened seals of virginity at His Birth, so He passed through the unopened seals of the tomb: ὥσπερ γὰρ ἐσφραγισμένων τῶν πανεμφύτων μητρανοίκτων κλείθρων τῆς παρθενικῆς φύσεως Χριστὸς ἐκ παρθένου γεγέννηται· οὕτως ἀδιανοίκτων ὄντων τῶν τοῦ τάφου σφραγίδων ἡ Χριστοῦ ἀναγέννησις πέπρακται[1]. But then there is a difference between the two great events, for while Christ did not break through the Virgin's gates, He burst through the gates of Hades: τὰς δὲ πύλας τῆς παρθένου μὴ διαρρήξας, ἀλλὰ πύλας τοῦ ᾅδου συντρίψας[2].

This fanciful parallelism is perhaps the explanation of the introduction of the topic of the Virgin Birth into Ode xix, where a detailed statement appears somewhat incongruously. The subject seems at first sight so alien to the thoughts of our Odist, that it has been supposed by some that Ode xix, or at any rate the second portion of it, is later than the body of our Hymns. But now that we know how closely the topics of Baptism, the Descent into Hades, and the Virgin Birth were connected in early Christian thought, we can understand that Ode xix 6 foll. may very well be contemporary and of identical authorship with the rest of the collection[3].

§ 20. *The interchange of speakers in the Odes.*

Of the 41 extant Odes, 25 seem to be spoken *ex ore catechumenorum*, viz. i, iii, iv, v, vi, vii, xi, xii, xiv, xvi, xviii, xix, xxi, xxiv, xxv, xxvi, xxvii, xxix, xxxii, xxxv, xxxvi, xxxvii, xxxviii, xl, xli. They express the personal joys and hopes of the soul that is entering upon its Divine inheritance. Six Odes are hortatory or didactic, viz. ix, xiii, xxiii, xxx, xxxiv, xxxix; and in these the song is placed in the mouth of the Church. In

[1] *l.c.* col. 444.   [2] *l.c.* col. 452.
[3] In a Maronite baptismal Ordo printed by Denzinger (*l.c.* I. 344), the three topics of the Virgin Birth, the Baptism of Christ, and His Descent into Hell, are brought together in a curious passage: "Ille igitur, voluntate sua, tua, ac spiritus sancti, habitavit in tribus mansionibus, in ventre carnis, et in sinu baptismi, atque in mansionibus inferni moerore plenis."

Ode x the Speaker is, apparently, Christ. There remain eight Odes, where it seems necessary to suppose a transition of personality. Odes viii, xxxi, and xxxiii begin with the Church's exhortation (viii 1—9, xxxi 1—6 and xxxiii 1—5), and pass—almost unconsciously—into the promises of God or Christ (viii 10—22, xxxi 7—end and xxxiii 6—end). Ode xxii which opens with words of Christ passes, at v 6, into the thanksgiving of the Christian. Ode xx begins with the confession of the baptized (xx 1—2), and then the theme is taken up by the Church (xx 3—end). Ode xxviii begins in like manner with the joy of the individual soul (xxviii 1—7), and ends with words of which Christ must be the speaker (xxviii 8—end). So Ode xlii 1—3 is spoken by the believer, but from v 4 to the end, the words are the words of Christ. The same may be said of Ode xvii, where perhaps the division comes at the end of v 10; and also of Ode xv. But if we may read "His Word" for "my word" at v 9, as Dr Harris suggests, Ode xv would be a personal hymn throughout. In all these cases there is room for doubt as to where the break comes; for the union of the believer with Christ, and his incorporation in the Church, are taken as certain, so that what the Church says might not unfitly be placed in the mouth of the believer, who is again a member of Christ (xvii 14)[1].

The dialogue form, or interchange of persons, is a common feature in the hymns of Ephraim Syrus, so that we need not be surprised at its appearance in our Odes[2].

§ 21. *The "Adversaries" of the Odist.*

The warfare to which the Odist refers again and again is the spiritual combat, and the adversaries who are most in his thoughts are the spiritual forces of evil.

---

[1] Cyril says of the baptized that having become partakers of Christ, they are "properly called Christs," and that they have been made Christs by receiving the antitype of the Holy Ghost (*Cat.* xxi. 1).

[2] Grimme distinguishes between the "I" Odes, in which the first person singular is used, and the "We" Odes, in which the plural form occurs; and actually marks off all the "We" sections as Christian interpolations (*l.c.* p. 128). But this is arbitrary criticism.

The persecutors of Christ were, indeed, men of flesh and blood; and Ode xxviii 8—end speaks of His persecutions by the Jews and in His Passion, while Ode xlii 5 is the word of His triumph, "All my persecutors are dead." It is possible, though not quite certain (see notes), that Ode xlii 7 and Ode xxiii 13—18 speak in like manner of the persecution of Christians by the Church's foes, and the Church's victory.

But the "war" of Ode viii 8 and Ode ix 7 is the spiritual campaign to which the baptized are pledged. Ode xxxviii 10 f. may carry (see note) an allusion to Antichrist and the temptations with which he will assail the Church; but these, too, are of a spiritual sort. Perhaps Ode xxv 3, 5 and Ode vi 9 (see note) may contemplate the earthly enemies of the Gospel; but the victory of Ode vi 3, 4 and Ode xxix 10 is clearly a spiritual victory. So, too, the imprecations upon persecutors that are found in Ode v 4 f. refer to the demonic forces which assail the Christian soul.

§ 22. *The Unity of Authorship.*

The style and manner of the Odist are the same throughout. He dwells continually on the same themes, *e.g.* *Love* (see on Ode v 1), *Knowledge* (see on vi 5), *Truth* (see on viii 9), *Faith* (see on iv 5), *Joy* (see on vii 1), *Hope* (see on v 9), *Rest* (see on iii 6), *Light* (see on xv 3), *Fruit* (see on viii 3), *Peace* (see on viii 8), *Redemption* (see on x 3). *Grace* (see on v 3) is much in his thoughts, and the *Putting on of Christ* (see on vii 6). These are all topics specially appropriate to the instruction offered to catechumens as they entered upon their new responsibilities in baptism, as will be shewn in detail in the notes to the Odes.

So, too, we should observe the frequency with which *crowns* or *garlands* are mentioned (see on Ode i 1); the references to *water*, and the thirst of the soul for the water of life (see on vi 10), and the number of passages in which the Christian is compared to a *harp* on which the Spirit plays (see on vi 1).

§ 23. *Conclusion.*

The conclusion which seems to the present writer to emerge most clearly from an examination of the Odes is, as has been said, that they are baptismal hymns intended for use in public worship, either for catechumens or for those who have recently been baptized. This view will be justified in detail in the annotations which are appended to each Ode. A few parallelisms here and there might be set down to chance, but when we find that this scheme of interpretation, applied to every Ode, provides a consistent explanation of their phraseology in every case, and in some cases illuminates obscure phrases for which no other explanation has been suggested, we are entitled to claim for it serious consideration. The strength of the argument depends upon its cumulative character. This view of their origin and meaning has the additional advantage, that it takes the Odes as they stand and is not dependent upon theories of interpolation, by which all inconvenient phrases may be set aside.

It is hardly less clear that the Odes are of Syrian, or Palestinian, origin. The baptismal allusions which abound are always to beliefs or practices current in the East; with Western doctrine or Western ceremonial they have little affinity. The best commentary upon them is Denzinger's invaluable collection of Eastern baptismal rites[1], to which repeated reference will be made.

As to their date, inasmuch as they are cited by the end of the third century as Scripture, they can hardly be later than 200 A.D., and may be some years earlier. But the apocryphal additions to the story of the Birth of Christ (Ode xix), and the elaborated Christology which appears once or twice (Ode xxxii), forbid us to put them earlier than 150 A.D. We do not know much of the development of the baptismal ritual in the second century, but it is not likely that it was so fully organised as it appears to be in these Odes, before the days of Justin Martyr. I incline, then, to a date between 150 and 200 for their origin, and preferably in the latter half of that period.

I have not attempted to discuss at length the original language of the Odes, a task demanding special linguistic qualifications

---

[1] Denzinger, *Ritus Orientalium*, vol. I. (Würzburg, 1863).

which I cannot claim; but, as indicated in § 6, the arguments in favour of a Semitic original, Syriac or Aramaic, seem to me to be stronger than those which are alleged on the side of Greek.

No new translation is here offered. By the great generosity of my friend Dr Rendel Harris I am permitted to use his admirable rendering of the Syriac text of which he was the discoverer and first editor. I have not followed it at every point, and have freely used the alternative renderings of Burkitt, Flemming, Labourt, and Schultess, wherever they seemed to yield a more convincing sense without unduly departing from the text. But I could not have undertaken the task of commenting on the Odes, had it not been for the kindness of Dr Harris in sanctioning the use generally of his translation, while he is not, of course, in any way responsible either for the alterations which I have introduced into it, or for the inferences which I have derived from the words of the Odist.

TRANSLATION AND NOTES

ODE I.

¹The Lord is on my head like a crown, and I shall not be without Him. ²A crown of truth has been woven* for me, and it has caused thy shoots to grow in me. ³For it is not like a withered crown which blossometh not; but thou livest upon my head, and thou hast blossomed upon my head. ⁴Thy fruits are full grown and perfect, full of thy salvation.

This Ode is not extant in the Syriac version, the manuscript of which is defective at the beginning, but it is cited in *Pistis Sophia*, as was discovered by the sagacity of Harris. It is reckoned as Ode xix in that treatise, but Harris has identified it convincingly with Ode i, according to the reckoning of the Syriac MS. He points out that in the collection of these poems known to the author of *Pistis Sophia*, the 18 "Psalms" must have preceded the 42 "Odes," instead of following them as they do in his Syriac version.

Allusions to *crowns* are frequent in the Odes; cp. Odes v 10, ix 8 f., xvii 1, xx 7. The significance of the allusion is revealed by a study of the Eastern baptismal rites, which in several instances prescribe the ceremony of crowning the neophyte with garlands or chaplets. In the rite which bears the name of Severus, the Monophysite Patriarch of Antioch (512–519 A.D.), we find the rubric *et sertis coronat eos*†, and this is followed by a hymn ‡ which contains the words *coronas haud marcescentes, fratres, accepistis* (cp. v. 3). Another *Ordo* called after Severus§ has a phrase even closer to our Ode: *coronam haud marcescibilem capiti tuo Dominus tuus, voces laudis attollit ei os tuum*. For *capiti tuo* we turn to vv. 1, 3. The same ceremony is found in the Armenian rite‖, in an *Ordo* of James of Edessa, and in Coptic and Aethiopic rituals¶. An earlier allusion appears in a hymn of

---

* The Coptic verb is the 3rd singular perfect passive, as Worrell points out (*l.c.* p. 34). Harris renders " they wove for me a crown of truth."
† Denzinger, *Ritus Orient.* I. 315.
‡ See above, p. 21.   § Denzinger, *l.c.* I. 309.
‖ Conybeare, *Rituale Armenorum*, pp. 99, 101.
¶ Denzinger, *l.c.* I. 288, 210, 221, 295, 231, 326, 349, 397.

Ephraim Syrus, cited above*: "Crowns that fade not away are set on your heads; hymns of praise hourly let your mouths sing."

Harris thinks that we have a yet earlier reminiscence of this crowning of the baptized in Hermas (*Sim.* VIII.), where stress is laid upon the fact that only martyrs were crowned, the inference being that, at some previous period, coronation with garlands was an ordinary baptismal ceremony. But this is, perhaps, precarious.

Attention has already been called to the remarkable similarity which the phraseology of this introductory Ode presents to the opening sentences of Cyril's *Procatechesis*, or introductory lecture to his catechumens; a similarity which would go far, by itself, to justify the baptismal character of the Ode (see p. 18).

There is a passage in Cant. iii 11 which is, perhaps, worth citing, in view of the fact that these Odes go by the name of Solomon:

> Go forth, O ye daughters of Zion, and behold king Solomon,
> With the crown wherewith his mother hath crowned him
>   in the day of his espousals,
> And in the day of the gladness of his heart.

Cyril of Jerusalem† interprets this crown of the Crown of Thorns at the Passion, and adds a curious comment: μυστήριον δὲ ἦν καὶ ὁ στέφανος, λύσις γὰρ ἦν τῶν ἁμαρτιῶν, ἀπόλυσις τῆς ἀποφάσεως. Cyril had alluded in a previous Lecture‡ to the baptismal crown or garland, by quoting Isa. lxi 10 "He hath crowned me with a garland, as a bridegroom"; and when he speaks of the "crown" of Cant. iii 11 as "the remission of sins," the suspicion is aroused that he may be thinking of that "one baptism for the remission of sins," which is the climax of all his catechetical instruction. If it could be shewn that the crowning of Solomon, spoken of in Cant. iii 11, was interpreted mystically of baptism, we might have a clue to the attribution of the whole collection of Odes (which begin with the thought of crowns and come back to it many times) to Solomon as their author §.

Ode II. [missing].

Ode III.

......I put on: ²and his members are with him. And on them do I hang, and He loves me: ³for I should not have known how to love the Lord, if He had not loved me. ⁴For who is able to distinguish love, except the one that is loved? ⁵I love the

* p. 20.
† *Cat.* XIII. 17. ‡ *Cat.* III. 2.
§ But see Introd. § 9. The absence of parallels to the Song of Songs in the Odes is noteworthy.

Beloved, and my soul loves Him*: ⁶and where His rest is, there also am I; ⁷and I shall be no stranger, for with the Lord Most High and Merciful there is no grudging. ⁸I have been united to Him, for the Lover has found the Beloved, ⁹and because I shall love Him that is the Son, I shall become a son; ¹⁰for he that is joined to Him that is immortal, will also himself become immortal; ¹¹and he who has pleasure in life, will become living. ¹²This is the Spirit of the Lord, which doth not lie, which teacheth the sons of men to know His ways. ¹³Be wise and understanding and vigilant. Hallelujah.

v. 2. The "members" of Christ are mentioned again, Ode xvii 14.

v. 3. Cp. 1 John iv 19; the phrase betrays the influence of Johannine thoughts, if not actually a knowledge of the Fourth Gospel.

v. 5. "Mystical union and spiritual love" are the keynotes of this Ode, as Mr Aytoun says. He compares a passage from the ninth century *Exposition of Baptism* by Moses bar Kepha: "The betrothals of Rebecca, Rachel, and Zipporah, were beside water. So also are the betrothals of the Holy Church beside the waters of baptism †."

v. 6. The reference to the Lord's "rest" is significant, and it is one of several which appear in the Odes. Cp. Odes xi 10, xx 8, xxvi 13, xxviii 4, xxx 2, xxxvi 1, xxxvii 4, and xxxviii 4. The clue to this is found in the fact that the baptismal waters were regarded as "waters of rest" with allusion to Ps. xxii (xxiii) 2‡. Hence our Odist calls his poems "the Odes of the Lord's rest" (Ode xxvi 3). Clement of Alexandria has the phrases: "As soon as we are regenerated, we are honoured by receiving the good news of the hope of rest"; and again, "where faith is, there is the promise; and the consummation of the promise is rest. So that in Illumination [sc. Baptism] what we receive is knowledge and the end of knowledge is rest §." But the difference between him and our Odist is that while for Clement baptism only gives the hope of rest as the final consummation, rest is treated in the Odes as already the portion of the baptized. See also on Odes xxx 2 and xlii 8.

v. 8. Cp. Rom. vi 5 for union with Christ in baptism.

v. 9. Cp. Gal. iv 5 for the "adoption of sons."

v. 10. The idea that baptism, by incorporating the neophyte with the Living Christ, makes him a sharer in Christ's immortality is familiar. "Being baptized" says Clement‖ "we are illuminated; illuminated we become

---

* Labourt suggests an emendation of the text, which preserves the parallelism: "my soul is loved by Him."

† § 16 quoted in *Expositor*, Oct. 1911, p. 344.

‡ Theodoret interprets the ὕδωρ ἀναπαύσεως of Ps. xxii (xxiii) 2, of baptism; and Jerome does the same (*Anecd. Maredsolana*, III. iii. 124).

§ *Paed.* I. 6 (115, 116 P). ‖ *Paed.* I. 6 (113 P).

sons; being made sons we are made perfect; being made perfect we are made immortal." Ephraim has a similar thought although his language is not so close as Clement's to that of our Odist: "Go down to the Fountain of Christ, and receive life in your members, as armour against death*."

v. 11. Harris emends the text so as to read: "he who has pleasure in the Living One," and compares Rev. i 17 as illustrating this title of Christ. But the MS. reading gives quite good sense, and it is to be remembered that the Apocalypse was no part of the primitive Syriac Canon†.

Ode IV.

¹No man, O my God, changeth thy holy place; ²and it is not [possible] that he should change it and put it in another place; because he hath no power over it: ³for thy sanctuary thou hast designed before thou didst make places: ⁴that which is the elder shall not be altered by those that are younger than itself. ⁵Thou hast given thy heart, O Lord, to thy believers: never wilt thou fail, nor be without fruits: ⁶for one hour of thy Faith is more precious than all days and years. ⁷For who is there that shall put on thy grace, and be hurt? ⁸For thy seal is known: and thy creatures know it: and thy hosts possess it: and the elect archangels are clad with it. ⁹Thou hast given us thy fellowship: it was not that thou wast in need of us: but that we are in need of thee: ¹⁰distil thy dews upon us and open thy rich fountains that pour forth to us milk and honey: ¹¹for there is no repentance with thee that thou shouldest repent of anything that thou hast promised: ¹²and the end was revealed before thee: for what thou gavest, thou gavest freely: ¹³so that thou mayest not draw them back and take them again: ¹⁴for all was revealed before thee as God, and ordered from the beginning before thee: and thou, O God, hast made all things. Hallelujah.

vv. 1—4. This is a difficult Ode, and the character and date of the whole collection will be determined, to some extent, by the interpretation that we place upon it. Harris and Harnack hold that the allusion in *vv.* 1—4 is to the Jewish Temple; and Harris claims that according to Rabbinical teaching the Temple was prior to all created things‡. Harris finds in *v.* 1 a further

* *Epiphany Hymns*, vii. 17.

† Cp. however, Ode xxxviii 10 f. and *Introd.* p. 28.

‡ Bacon, however, points out that "the Sanctuary" in the passage cited by Harris from *Pirke Aboth* is not the Temple, but the Promised Land (*Expositor*, Mar. 1911, p. 202).

allusion to some unsuccessful attempt to alter the site of the "Holy Place," and perhaps to the closing of the Temple at Leontopolis in Egypt. He would therefore date the Ode shortly after 73 A.D. Harnack, on the other hand, thinks that the Temple at Leontopolis as well as the Temple at Jerusalem was still standing, and therefore he considers the Ode to be prior to 70 A.D. Both scholars agree that the writer was a Jew, if not by race, at all events by sympathy. And in his second edition* Harris quotes a comment of Philo's on Exod. xv 17 which, in his view, connects *vv.* 1—4 with *v.* 9. The passage in Exodus is:

"Thou shalt bring them in, and plant them in the mountain of thine inheritance,

"The place, O Lord, which thou hast made for thee to dwell in,

"The sanctuary, O Lord, which thy hands have established.

"The Lord shall reign for ever and ever."

Philo interprets this not, however, of the Temple, but of the higher life of man, which is called the mountain of the Lord's inheritance, and reverts to his doctrine that the sanctuary is an imitation of the heavenly archetype, adding: "but in order that no one may suppose that the Creator is in need of any of the things that have come into being, he subjoins the most necessary phrase 'King for ever and ever.' For a king is in need of nothing, but the things subject to a king are all under law†."

Now in the first place if the reference to the Jewish Temple in *vv.* 1—4 be substantiated, we have here a phenomenon which does not present itself again throughout the whole collection of Odes, viz. a reference to definite times and localities. The singer praises God in all the other Odes *sub specie aeternitatis*; his songs are timeless; his thought is not bounded by the condition of the country in which his lot is cast. And, moreover, such a view of *vv.* 1—4 accords very ill with what follows; there is, apparently, no connexion at all with *v.* 5: "One hour of thy Faith is more precious than all days and years. For who is there that shall put on thy grace, and be hurt?" Nor is there any appositeness to be discerned in the mention of a "seal" in *v.* 6, or of the "milk and honey" in *v.* 10.

Again, the idea that God needs nothing, while we need Him, which is found in Philo in connexion with Exod. xv 17, is a commonplace in early Christian literature, as Harris himself points out‡. Irenaeus in successive chapters§ repeats it again and again. God is not in need of man whom He created, or of his service or obedience; He did not need the tabernacle or the temple or any of the sacrifices or ordinances of the Levitical dispensation, nor does he need the offerings of Christians. "Ipse quidem nullius indigens; his vero qui indigent eius, suam praebens communionem." But this is not a specially Jewish idea; like many Christian ideas, it is inherited from, or has its roots in, Judaism, but it is not peculiar to Judaism;

---

* p. xxviii. † *De Plantatione*, § 12.
‡ p. 93; op. Acts xvii 25. § *Adv. Haer.* IV. 14—18.

and that God has given man His fellowship (v. 9) is a thought much more clearly expressed in Christian than in Jewish teaching.

Conybeare, who finds traces of Montanism in the Odes, has suggested that by the "holy place" of verse 1 is indicated Pepuza in Phrygia, where the Montanists declared that the New Jerusalem had descended*. And Fries, in a later article†, takes a similar view, preferring however to identify the unchangeable sanctuary with a little Phrygian town called Tymion. Apart from my inability to find any sure traces of Montanism in the Odes, these interpretations seem to me to be beset by the same difficulty as that to which the theories of Harris and Harnack are exposed, viz. that the tone of Ode iv does not suggest that the singer is thinking of a definite locality.

Origen interprets the sanctuary of Exod. xv 17‡ as typifying the Incarnation. "Audi sapientiam dicentem quia *aedificavit sibi domum* (Prov. ix 1). Ego autem hoc de incarnatione Domini rectius intelligendum puto." This is not in question here, for the thought of our Odist is rather of the unique dignity of the *Church*, the company of the baptized. There is no allusion, as it seems to me, to the buildings of the Jewish Temple. The Holy Place of v. 1 is not the material sanctuary, but the Church in its eternal being, subsisting in the Divine Idea. It is to be observed that the word "other" which Harris supplies before "places" in v. 3, has no counterpart in the original Syriac. The literal translation is "thy sanctuary thou hast designed before thou didst make places," *i.e.* the Sanctuary of the Church existed in the Divine counsels before "places" were made at the Creation.

This idea is explicit in Hermas§. Hermas asks who is the aged woman of his vision, and the answer is "the Church." "Wherefore then is she aged?" Hermas asks, and he is told "because she was created before all things; therefore is she aged, and for her sake the world was framed" (...Ἡ ἐκκλησία, φησίν· εἶπον αὐτῷ· Διατί οὖν πρεσβυτέρα; Ὅτι, φησίν, πάντων πρώτη ἐκτίσθη· διὰ τοῦτο πρεσβυτέρα, καὶ διὰ ταύτην ὁ κόσμος κατηρτίσθη).

Again, Clement of Alexandria says that heresies are innovations on the oldest Church, unity being a characteristic of the Church which is true and ancient. It stands alone, μίμημα ὂν ἀρχῆς τῆς μιᾶς∥. This is not so near to our Odist as Hermas, but it illustrates the prevalence of the idea of the Church's antiquity.

It may be added that Lactantius, more than once, speaks of the Church as "the true temple of God." "This is the faithful house (cf. 1 Sam. ii 35); this is the everlasting temple¶." And Narsai, the Syrian homilist, speaks in like manner: "Two several institutions [God] made in His wisdom...an earthly abode He called the earthly sanctuary; and a holy of holies He called that institution which is hidden in the height," sc. the Church**.

* *Zeitschrift für die N. T. Wissenschaft*, 1911, p. 74.
† *l.c.* p. 115.
‡ *Hom. in Exod.* vi 12.   § *Vis.* II. 4.
∥ *Strom.* VII. 107.   ¶ *Div. Inst.* iv 13, 14.
** *Hom.* XXXII. (D), p. 62, ed. Connolly.

ODE IV

We observe next the language of a prayer for the catechumens in a Jacobite baptismal *Ordo*, which is thus translated: "Planta eos in monte haereditatis tuae, in praeparato habitaculo tuo quod praeparasti Domine, in sanctuario quod praepararunt manus tuae*." Undoubtedly in this prayer, the sanctuary which God's hands have prepared is the Church, foreshadowed and typified in the hymn of Exod. xv 17. Indeed the priest proceeds shortly afterwards to say: "Planta eos ut veram plantam in sancta catholica ecclesia." To Christian exegesis the sanctuary is the Promised Land of the Church, which is reached when the people, like Israel of old, have passed through the waters. And it is this which the unchangeable sanctuary of v. 1 signifies—the ancient Church, pre-existent in God's counsels, before the creation of material things, not to be set aside in favour of any younger institution—the Church to which the neophyte is admitted by the baptismal washing.

v. 5. The Baptized were called πιστοί, *believers*, in contradistinction to the Catechumens, and were expected to exhibit the fruit of the Spirit. Cp. Ode xxii 7. So Cyril says: Πρὸ τούτου κατηχούμενος ἦς, νῦν δὲ κληθήσῃ πιστός......ἐὰν μὲν ἐπιμείνῃς ἐν τῇ ἀμπέλῳ αὔξῃ, ὡς κλῆμα καρποφόρον... καρποφορήσωμεν τοίνυν ἀξίως†. This is exactly the sequence of thought in this verse.

For other references to *faith* see Odes viii 12, xvi 5, xxviii 4, xxix 6, xxxix 11, xli 1, xlii 12.

vv. 7, 8. The protective grace of baptism is the thought here (see on Ode v 3); it is as a seal which the heavenly hosts recognise.

It is unnecessary to multiply references for the expression "seal" as applied to baptism, but it appears as early as Hermas‡. See Ode viii 16.

If the words of *v.* 8 "the elect archangels are clad with it," represent exactly the original text (and this is always doubtful in the case of a reading preserved only in one late manuscript), they are difficult to interpret on any hypothesis, Jewish or Christian. It is true that there was a doctrine current among the Valentinian sect§ that angels were recipients of baptism, but there is no probability that any allusion to this is to be found here. It is more likely that the thought is that the splendour of baptismal grace is like the splendours of the heavenly host, as in the following Hymn "On the Baptized," which appears among the hymns of Severus of Antioch, and may be quoted in full at this point: "When I look at the children of the laver of regeneration, I turn the glances of my eyes downwards; for an ethereal spiritual savour has alighted and sat upon their head, and *splendour such as befits the holy host on high;* which if they keep they shall dwell in eternal

---

* Denzinger, *Rit. Orient.* I. 270. The same prayer is found in the *Ordo* of Severus of Antioch (*l.c.* I. 310).

† *Cat.* I. 4 (cp. v. 1).

‡ *Sim.* IX. 16 (a section from which the word βαπτισμός is absent, just as it is from our Odes); cp. 2 Clem. 8, and Ephraim, *Epiphany Hymns*, IX. 6, and *passim*.

§ See Clem. Alex. *Exc. Theodot.* 22.

habitations, when pain and sorrow and sighing have fled away, as it is written, praising Christ for His great mercy*." The tone and character of this short hymn, it should be noticed, are very similar to what we find in the Odes.

The same thought is found, in terser language, in Gregory Nazianzen's Oration on Baptism †: "In it [*i.e.* the seal] the heavens rejoice; *it is glorified by angels because of its kindred splendour.*"

There is, however, a passage in the Catechetical Lectures of Cyril of Jerusalem which is so like the phrasing of *v.* 8, that it suggests another meaning for the word translated "are clad," or perhaps a corruption of the text. Cyril is speaking‡ of the gift of baptism: Τὴν σωτηριώδη δίδωσι σφραγίδα τὴν θαυμασίαν, ἣν τρέμουσι δαίμονες καὶ γινώσκουσιν ἄγγελοι. Cyril's thought is that the hosts of heaven and hell recognise the power of the baptismal seal. We have the same thing in Basil's Homily on Baptism (§ 4). There is no need, Basil says, to despair because of sin, because grace abounds. If demons draw men to evil, angels draw them to good. And as to soldiers a *tessera* is given that their friends may recognize them in the battle, so is it in the spiritual combat. Baptism is the seal, without which hardly will heavenly guardians be able to recognize the Christian soldier. Πῶς ἀντιποιηθῇ σου ὁ ἄγγελος; πῶς δὲ ἀφέληται τῶν ἐχθρῶν, ἐὰν μὴ ἐπιγνῷ τὴν σφραγίδα; πῶς δὲ σὺ ἐρεῖς, Τοῦ θεοῦ εἰμί, μὴ ἐπιφερόμενος τὰ γνωρίσματα; Basil says the same thing again in his 8th Sermon on Penitence (§ 5); angels recognise the baptismal seal, οὐδεὶς ἐπιγνώσεταί σε......ἐὰν μὴ τοῖς μυστικοῖς συμβόλοις παράσχῃ τὴν οἰκειότητα κ.τ.λ. Here, then, we have exactly the thought of *vv.* 7, 8: the "seal" which is "known" by the angels is the seal of heaven and its protecting grace. So too in one of the Syriac Hymns of Severus of Antioch mention is made of "the angels dancing and singing praise in spiritual companies and bands, over the salvation of those who have been baptized and enlightened §." Another illustration may be found in a baptismal *Ordo* of James of Edessa‖, where we find: "Exercitus caelestium circumadstat baptisterio, ut ex aquis suscipiant filios deo similes," words which express the similar idea of the interest of the angels in the act of initiation ¶.

v. 9. We proceed to the next verse, and we find again words entirely appropriate to the thought of the baptism of Christ, by which His fellowship with man was specially asserted. "I have need to be baptized of thee, and comest thou to me?" was the question of the Baptist (Matt. iii 14). But Christ was baptized nevertheless, says Epiphanius**, ἵνα δείξῃ, ὅτι ἀληθινὴν

---

* Patr. Orient. VI. i. p. 134.   † § 4.
‡ Cat. I. 3.   § Patr. Orient. VI. i. p. 137.
‖ Denzinger, *l.c.* I. 287 and Assemani, *Cod. Liturg.* II. 226; cp. Cosmas, *l.c.* 470.
¶ Cp. Cyr. Hier. Procat. 15 ἤδη μοι χοροὺς ἀγγελικοὺς ἐννοήσατε...θρόνους δὲ καὶ κυριότητας λειτουργοῦντας: see also Tert. *de Baptismo,* 4, 6.
** Anaceph. 1136.

ODE IV

σάρκα ἐνεδύσατο, ἀληθινὴν ἐνανθρώπησιν, κατερχόμενος εἰς τὰ ὕδατα, διδοὺς ἧπερ λαμβάνων, παρεχόμενος ἧπερ ἐπιδεόμενος κ.τ.λ. This is very close to: "not that thou wast in need of us, but that we are in need of thee."

In a Hymn of Severus of Antioch for the Epiphany*, Christ is similarly described as "He that lacketh not, as one that lacketh, and was named the Second Adam, because in all things a beginning to us."

v. 10. "Distil thy dews upon us." "Dew" is mentioned again Ode xi 13 and Ode xxxv 1; it is a common description of baptism. Basil speaks of baptism as δρόσος ψυχῆς†, and Lactantius says‡ that as Christ saved the Jews by being circumcised, so He saves the Gentiles by baptism, *i.e.* "by the perfusion of the purifying dew." So Ephraim sings "With thy dew besprinkle my vileness §."

"Open Thy rich fountains that pour forth to us milk and honey." There are many traces in early Christian literature from the second century onward of a rite of administering milk and honey to the newly baptized, to symbolize their entrance into "the land flowing with milk and honey," the land of promise which the chosen people reached after passing through the waters of Jordan. We have it mentioned twice in Tertullian: "Inde suscepti lactis et mellis concordiam praegustamus" (*De Cor.* 3) and "Deus mellis et lactis societate suos infantat" (*adv. Marc.* i. 14). Tertullian says that the rite was practised by the Marcionites, so that it must go back to the middle of the second century at any rate‖. See note on Ode viii 17, and for other references to *milk*, Odes xix 1, xxxv 6.

v. 11. The gift of God is inalienable, cp. Rom. xi 29. With the thoughts of *vv.* 9, 1, 14, 11 may be compared the phrases of a prayer in the Apostolical Constitutions (vii 35): "Thou...whose life is without want...whose dwelling is unchangeable (ἀμετανάστευτος ἡ κατασκήνωσις), whose knowledge is without beginning, whose truth is immutable."

v. 12. "What thou gavest, thou gavest freely." Cyril notes, in like manner, the freedom of the baptismal gift: "Despise not the grace because it is freely given" is his counsel ¶.

v. 14. Loisy points out that, just as *v.* 3 declares that God has designed His sanctuary from eternity, so *v.* 14 declares that the spiritual gifts which He provides have been fore-ordained from the beginning**. The Ode is thus entirely consistent with itself, and forms a complete whole, the key to the understanding of it being the recognition of the "holy place" as no earthly temple but as the mystical home of believers. Wellhausen agrees with this

---

* *Patr. Orient.* vi. i. p. 58.　　　　　† *Hom.* xiii. 2.
‡ *Div. Inst.* iv. 15.　　　　　§ *Epiphany Hymns* v. 15.
‖ See also *Egypt. Ch. Ord.* can. 46; *Can. Hippol.* xix; *Concil. Carthag.* iii. can. 24; Jerome, *ad Lucifer.* Opp. ii. 180 and *in Esai.* lv. The rite is still retained in Abyssinia (Denzinger, *Rit. Orient.* i. p. 232). Probably another reference may be found in Ephraim, *Rhythm.* xxii. 1 (ed. Morris, p. 178).
¶ *Cat.* i. 4.
** *Zeitschrift für N. T. Wissenschaft*, 1911, p. 126.

view of the Ode; while he does not profess to explain its opening phrases, he says that he believes "dass das unwandelbare Heiligtum hinterher als die von Ewigkeit prädestinierte Gemeinschaft der Gläubigen aufgefasst wird, in der Gott wohnt, wie in Ode 6 und 28*." Neither Loisy nor Wellhausen, however, has observed that it is the Church as the home of the baptized which is behind the singer's words of hope and joy.

Ode V.

¹I will give thanks unto thee, O Lord, because I love thee†; ²O most High, thou wilt not forsake me, for thou art my hope: ³freely I have received thy grace, I shall live thereby: ⁴My persecutors will come‡ and not see me: ⁵a cloud of darkness shall fall [on] their eyes; and an air of thick gloom shall darken them: ⁶and they shall have no light to see: that they may not take hold upon me. ⁷Let their counsel become powerless§, and what they have cunningly devised, let it return upon their own heads: ⁸for they have devised a counsel, and it did not succeed‖: they have prepared themselves for evil, and were found to be empty. ⁹For my hope is upon the Lord, and I will not fear, and because the Lord is my salvation, I will not fear: ¹⁰and He is as a garland on my head and I shall not be moved; even if everything should be shaken, I stand firm; ¹¹and if all things visible should perish, I shall not die: because the Lord is with me and I am with Him. Hallelujah.

This Ode is one of those quoted in *Pistis Sophia*.

v. 1. Allusions to the love of God are frequent in the Odes; cp. Odes iii 2 f., viii 2, 14, 23, xi 2, xii 11, xvi 4, xviii 1, xxiii 3, and see also Ode x 7.

v. 3. Allusions to "grace," *i.e.* (generally) the grace of baptism, are also frequent; cp. Odes iv 7, ix 5, xi 1, xv 8, xx 7, xxi 1, xxiii 2, xxv 4, xxxiii 1, xxxiv 6 and see also Ode vii 12, 25.

v. 9. "The Lord is my hope"; cp. Ode xxix 1.

v. 10. For the "garland" or baptismal chaplet, see on Ode i.

---

* *Göttingische gelehrte Anzeigen*, 1910, p. 639.
† The Coptic has "because Thou art my God."
‡ The mood in these verses may be optative.
§ So the Coptic. The Syriac word is obscure; Harris translates it "thick darkness."
‖ The Coptic has here the additional clause: "and they were overcome, although they were powerful."

v. 11. For the thought that union with the Lord is the pledge of immortality, see on Ode iii.

The adversaries of the Odist, for whose discomfiture he prays in *vv.* 4—8, are not men of flesh and blood; they are the spiritual foes of the Christian. See *Introd.* p. 40; but cp. also Ode xxiii 18.

Ode VI.

¹ As the hand moves over the harp, and the strings speak, ² so speaks in my members the Spirit of the Lord, and I speak by His love. ³ For it destroys what is alien, and everything is of the Lord: ⁴ for thus it was from the beginning and will be to the end, that nothing should be His adversary, and nothing should stand up against Him. ⁵ The Lord has multiplied the knowledge of Himself, and is zealous that these things should be known, which by His grace have been given to us. ⁶ And the praise of His Name he gave us: our spirits praise His holy Spirit. ⁷ For there went forth a stream, and became a river great and broad; ⁸ for it flooded and broke up everything, and it brought to the temple*: ⁹ and the restrainers of the children of men were not able to restrain it†, nor the arts of those whose business it is to restrain waters; ¹⁰ for it spread over the face of the whole earth, and filled everything; and all the thirsty upon earth were given to drink of it; ¹¹ and thirst was relieved and quenched: for from the Most High the draught was given. ¹² Blessed then are the ministers of that draught who are entrusted with that water of His: ¹³ they have assuaged the dry lips, and the will that had fainted they have raised up‡; ¹⁴ and souls that were near departing they have caught back from death: ¹⁵ and limbs that had fallen they straightened and set up: ¹⁶ they gave strength for their coming§ and light to their eyes. ¹⁷ for everyone knew them in the Lord, and they lived by the water of life for ever‖. Hallelujah.

* The Coptic has "It carried away all things, and it turned towards the temple."
† The Coptic has: "It could not be restrained by means of firm (dams) and built places."
‡ The Coptic has: "those who were exhausted have received joy of heart."
§ The Coptic has παρρησία here. See note *in loc.*
‖ The Coptic has: "they have saved themselves by water of eternal life."

A large part of this Ode, also, is preserved in *Pistis Sophia*—a fortunate circumstance, as it presents some special difficulties to the translator.

v. 1. That the Christian singer is, as it were, a harp played upon by the Holy Spirit, is an idea that appears again in the Odes; see xiv 8 and xxvi 3*. Some scholars have seen traces of Montanism in this, pressing the *passivity* of the harp in the hands of him who plays upon it. But such language as we have here is often found in orthodox Syrian writers. Thus Narsai, the Syriac homilist, was called by his friends the "Harp of the Holy Spirit"; and we find the image frequently in Ephraim's Hymns: "As the harp waiteth for its master, my mouth waiteth for thee"; "Blessed be he who becomes the harp of thy praise"; "My feeble tongue has become a harp through His mercy"; "The Harp of the Spirit they hushed which sang again of His Kingdom†." And again in Ephraim's Rhythms: "Do thou, Lord, play on my harp with all thy edifying strains"; "let thy Church also be a harp to thy praise‡." The various mystical senses of a harp are expounded by Clement of Alexandria in his *Stromata* (VI. 88). There is no heretical suggestion in the use of the image, which—as has been noted above—was specially prevalent among Syriac writers.

v. 3. For the words "everything is of the Lord," Harris prefers to emend the text and read "everything that is bitter." But as *vv.* 3, 4 stand in the original, they make good sense: the Spirit of the Lord is irresistible, and all that is alien to its nature is annulled.

v. 4. "Thus it was from the beginning and will be to the end": cp. Odes vii 17 and xi 4.

v. 5. There are many allusions in the Odes to the knowledge of God with which the singer has been favoured; cp. Odes vii 4, 24, viii 13, xi 4, xii 3, xv 5, xxiii 4. It was the special aim of the instruction of catechumens, that this highest knowledge should be imparted to them, in virtue of which the baptized are those who are being enlightened, $\phi\omega\tau\iota\zeta\acute{o}\mu\epsilon\nu o\iota$, *illuminati.*

v. 6. "The praise of His Name." See on Ode viii 22.

v. 7. This is the torrent § of the baptismal waters, typified by the river of Ezek. xlvii, which flowed out from under the Temple and, gathering volume in its progress, bore onward the waters of healing and fruitfulness. The water of this river appears in the LXX of Ezek. xlvii 3 as $\mathring{v}\delta\omega\rho$ $\mathring{a}\phi\acute{\epsilon}\sigma\epsilon\omega s$ "the water of remission," and many of the early Christian writers interpret it of the water of baptism. For instance, the following may be quoted from the *Sibylline Oracles*‖:

---

* Cp. also Tertullian, *de Bapt.* 8 "Deo autem in suo organo [sc. man] non licebit per manus sanctas sublimitatem modulari spiritalem."

† *Hymns on the Nativity*, X. XIV. XV. XVII.; cp. also II. and *Nisibene Hymns*, XIX. 8.

‡ Rhythm, XXI, Morris, *Select Works of Ephraim*, pp. 175, 177.

§ $\mathring{a}\pi\acute{o}\rho\rho o\iota a$ is the word reproduced in the Coptic *Pistis Sophia.*

‖ VI. 4 f.

ODE VI

.........προχοαῖς ἀπολουσάμενος ποταμοῖο
Ἰορδάνου, ὃς φέρεται γλαυκώπιδα κύματα σύρων,
ἐκ πυρὸς ἐκφεύξας πρῶτος θεοῦ ὄψεται ἠδὺ
πνεῦμ' ἐπιγινόμενον λευκῆς πτερύγεσσι πελειῆς·
ἀνθήσει δ' ἄνθος καθαρόν, βρύσουσι δὲ πηγαί.

The reference to Ezek. xlvii 12 is clear in this. Again, Barnabas quotes Ezek. xlvii 1, 7, 12 to typify the baptismal water*; and Melito of Sardes writes: οὕτω καὶ Ἰεζεκιὴλ ἐν τῷ τέλει ὕδωρ ἀφέσεως ἐκάλεσε τὸ ἐκτυποῦν τὸ ἅγιον βάπτισμα†. Of the commentators, Theodoret‡ and Jerome§ take the same line. Another pertinent reference is that of Ephraim Syrus in one of his Rhythms. Of Christ, he says: "Out of the stream whence the fishers came up [an obvious allusion to Ezek. xlvii 10] He was baptized and came up, who incloseth all things in His net‖." And probably another allusion is to be found in Ephraim's eleventh Epiphany hymn (v. 4): "Great was the mystery that the prophet saw, the torrent that was mighty. Into its depths he gazed and beheld thy beauty instead of himself; thee it was he saw, for thy faith passes not away, thou, whose flood unseen shall overwhelm the subtleties of idolatry." As late as the ninth century, Moses bar Kepha, in his Syriac *Exposition of Baptism* finds baptism typified in "the torrent which Ezekiel saw¶."

v. 8. Dr Harris, indeed, and Dr Harnack find in the language of the obscure verse 8 an indication of the Judaism of the writer, which might be thought to exclude baptismal thoughts; for the words "it flooded and broke up everything and it brought [all] to the Temple" are said to suggest that the goal of the life-giving stream is the Temple at Jerusalem. But this is only a reminiscence (even if the translation be trustworthy here) of the concluding words of the LXX of Ezek. xlvii 1, the passage on which the Odist is working, ἀπὸ νότου ἐπὶ τὸ θυσιαστήριον; and so it cannot be held as setting aside the interpretation which this *locus classicus* of the early Christian Fathers received from all who touched it.

v. 9. The "restrainers of waters" would seem to be the opponents of the

---

* § 11. Barnabas is here collecting O.T. *testimonia* to baptism, and he quotes Jer. ii 12 f. and Isa. xvi 1 and proceeds: καὶ πάλιν λέγει ὁ προφήτης· ἐγὼ πορεύσομαι ἔμπροσθέν σου· καὶ ὄρη ὁμαλιῶ καὶ πύλας χαλκᾶς συντρίψω καὶ μοχλοὺς σιδηροῦς συνκλάσω, καὶ δώσω σοι θησαυροὺς σκοτεινοὺς ἀποκρύφους, ἀοράτους...(Isa. xlv 2, 3). Next Isa. xxxiii 16—18 and Ps. i 3—6 are quoted, and finally he adds: εἶτα τί λέγει; καὶ ἦν ποταμὸς ἕλκων ἐκ δεξιῶν, καὶ ἀνέβαινεν ἐξ αὐτοῦ δένδρα ὡραῖα· καὶ ὃς ἂν φάγῃ, ἐξ αὐτῶν ζήσεται εἰς τὸν αἰῶνα (Ezek. xlvii 1, 7, 12; cp. John vi 51). τοῦτο λέγει ὅτι ἡμεῖς μὲν καταβαίνομεν εἰς τὸ ὕδωρ γέμοντες ἁμαρτιῶν καὶ ῥύπου, καὶ ἀναβαίνομεν καρποφοροῦντες ἐν τῇ καρδίᾳ κ.τ.λ. This passage is very important for the interpretation of the Odes.

† Routh, *Rel. Sacr.* I. 124.   ‡ *Comm. in Ezech.*
§ *Comm. in Ezech.*; cp. also Ep. lxix. *ad Oceanum.*
‖ Rhythm, III. (Morris, *Select Works of Ephraim*, p. 16).
¶ § 16 quoted by Aytoun, *Expositor*, Oct. 1911, p. 341.

Christian gospel. Gregory of Nyssa in his sermon *On the Baptism of Christ* uses a somewhat similar phrase. He has spoken of the wells digged by Isaac (Gen. xxvi 15 etc.) as a type of the baptismal waters, and he goes on: "...wells, which the aliens stopped and filled up, for a type of all those impious men of later days who hindered the grace of baptism, and talked loudly in their struggle against the truth. Yet the martyrs and the priests overcame them by digging the wells, and the gift of baptism overflowed the whole world," the last phrase being—it will be observed—almost identical with the opening words of *v.* 10 of our Ode.

vv. 10, 11. It might be urged as an objection to the interpretation of this water as baptismal, that the waters of Ezek. xlvii, interpreted by the Fathers of the waters of baptism, are waters of *healing* and *fruitfulness*, while the Living Water of the Odist is for *drinking*, a draught for the thirsty. And all through our Odes this is the purpose of the Water which the singer has in his thought. "Fill ye waters for yourselves from the living fountain of the Lord, for it is opened to you; and come all ye thirsty and take the draught and rest by the fountain of the Lord. For fair it is and pure, and gives rest to the soul. Much more pleasant are its waters than honey" are the opening words of Ode xxx. And more particularly in Ode xi 6 f.: "Speaking waters touched my lips from the fountain of the Lord plenteously, and I drank and was inebriated with the living water that doth not die." The Living Water of our Odes is represented as a life-giving *draught*. But however strange it may seem to us to think thus of the baptismal waters, the early interpreters of the Gospel were not so precise in their metaphors. We need not go beyond Ephraim, who presents at every point parallels to the thought of our Odes. In one of the baptismal hymns, to which allusion has frequently been made, he has a reference to the story of Num. xx 14—21, which tells how the Edomites refused Israel a passage through their territory, with the privilege of drinking at the wells: "To the sons of Lot, Moses said, 'Give us water for money, let us only pass by through your border.' They refused the way and the temporal water. Lo! the Living Water freely given and the path that leads to Eden*." And in the same hymn (at *v.* 21) Ephraim interprets the words of Christ to the Samaritan woman "Whoso drinketh of this water that I shall give him shall never thirst again" (John iv 14), as signifying mystically that baptism cannot be repeated—a fantastic comment, but apposite here to shew that the baptismal waters were conceived of by the early commentators as a draught for the thirsty, just as they are in our Odes†. See also on Ode xxx 1.

v. 12. "Blessed are the διάκονοι of that draught"—διάκονοι being the original word, as we see from its preservation in the rendering of *Pistis*

---

* *Epiphany Hymns*, vii. 7.

† Cp. Cyprian, *Ep.* lxiii. 8 "quotienscumque autem aqua sola in scripturis sanctis nominatur, baptisma praedicatur, ut apud Essaiam significari videmus": and he proceeds to quote and expound in this sense Isa. xliii 18—21, xlviii 21, John vii 37—39.

Sophia—may carry an allusion to the Christian deacons who administered baptism.

v. 13. If the Coptic has preserved the true text, we should compare Odes vii 1, xxiii 1, xxxii 1, for the joy of the Lord which the baptized soul experiences.

vv. 14, 15. There are similar expressions in other Odes, which seem, like these verses, to have reference to the supposed beneficial effect of baptism on the health of the body. "Sicknesses removed from my body" (Ode xviii 3); "my soul acquired a body free from sorrow or affliction" (Ode xxi 3); "thy right hand lifted me up and removed sickness from me" (Ode xxv 9). That such consequences not infrequently followed baptism was believed (*inter alios*) by Augustine*, and especially in Syria. Thus Narsai says, "With feeble waters he was pleased to confirm feeble bodies†"; and in a modern Nestorian office of baptism we find this thanksgiving: "Praise be unto Thee who hast healed the diseases of our bodies with the oil and water which thou hast poured into our wounds, and by thy Spirit as with a sponge hast wiped off the filth of sin from our souls‡." A rhetorical description of the spiritual and bodily effects of baptism may be quoted in full from Chrysostom, as a final illustration: "He first gave us the Washing, like some antidote, and thus we vomited up all our guilt, and all took its flight at once, and our inflammation ceased, and our fever was quenched, and our sores were dried up....Our eyes were opened, our ears were opened§, our tongue spake holy words: our soul received strength, our body received such beauty and bloom, as it is like that he who is born a son of God should have from the grace of the Spirit‖." This is very like the language of *vv.* 13—16. The ascent from the baptismal font was, in short, conceived to be, in Ezekiel's words, $ἀνάβασις$ $εἰς$ $ὑγίειαν$ (Ezek. xlvii 12).

v. 16. The Syriac is "they gave strength *for their coming*," while the Coptic rendering in *Pistis Sophia* has "they gave strength for their $παρρησία$." Harris ingeniously conjectures that $παρουσία$ (which he thinks to be behind the Syriac) and $παρρησία$ are both corruptions of $παράλυσις$ which he suggests as the original, comparing Isa. xxxv 3 and Heb. xii 12, and translates "they gave strength for their weakness." But "for their coming" gives a tolerable sense, and, as Grimme points out, it preserves better the parallelism of the first clause of the verse with the second.

---

* *De Civ. Dei* xxii. viii. 4, 5.
† *Hom.* xxii. (B) ed. Connolly, p. 41.
‡ Badger, *The Nestorians and their Rituals* ii. 200.
§ See the note on Ode viii 1 for the "opening of the ears."
‖ *Hom.* ii. *in Phil.* iii 12.

Ode VII.

¹ As the impulse of anger against iniquity, so is the impulse of joy towards the beloved (object); it brings in of its fruits without restraint: ² my joy is the Lord and my impulse is towards Him: this path of mine is excellent: ³ for I have a helper, the Lord. ⁴ He hath caused me to know Himself, without grudging, by His simplicity: His kindness hath humbled His greatness. ⁵ He became like me, in order that I might receive Him: ⁶ He was reckoned like myself in order that I might put Him on; ⁷ And I trembled not when I saw Him: because He was gracious to me: ⁸ like my nature He became that I might learn Him and like my form, that I might not turn back from Him: ⁹ the Father of Knowledge is the word of Knowledge: ¹⁰ He who created wisdom is wiser than His works: ¹¹ and He who created me when yet I was not, knew what I should do when I came into being: ¹² wherefore He pitied me in His abundant grace: and granted me to ask from Him and to receive from His sacrifice: ¹³ because He it is that is incorrupt, the fulness of the ages and the Father of them.

¹⁴ He hath given Him to be seen of them that are His, ¹⁵ in order that they may recognise Him that made them: and that they might not suppose that they came of themselves: ¹⁶ for knowledge He hath appointed as His way, He hath widened it and extended it; and brought it to all perfection; ¹⁷ and set over it the footprints of His light, and I walked ⌐therein⌐ from the beginning even to the end. ¹⁸ For by Him it was made, and it rested in the Son, and for His salvation He will take hold of everything: ¹⁹ and the Most High shall be known in His saints to proclaim the good news to those who have Songs of the Lord's Coming; ²⁰ that they may go forth to meet Him, and may sing to Him with joy and with the harp of many voices: ²¹ the seers shall come before Him and they shall be seen before Him, ²² and they shall praise the Lord for His love: because He is near and beholdeth, ²³ and hatred shall be taken from the earth, and along with jealousy it shall be drowned: ²⁴ for ignorance hath been destroyed, because the

knowledge of the Lord hath arrived. ²⁵ They who make songs shall sing the grace of the Lord Most High; ²⁶ and they shall bring their songs, and their heart shall be like the day: and like the excellent beauty of the Lord their pleasant song: ²⁷ and there shall neither be anything that breathes without knowledge, nor any that is dumb: ²⁸ for He hath given a mouth to His creation, to open the voice of the mouth towards Him, to praise Him: ²⁹ confess ye His power, and shew forth His grace. Hallelujah.

This is a Hymn of the Joy of the Lord. (Cp. Odes xxiii 1, xxxii·1.)

v. 3. For God as the "Helper" of man, cp. Odes viii 7, xxi 1, xxv 2.

For the knowledge of God, to which allusion is made in vv. 4, 16, 24, see on Ode vi 5.

vv. 4, 5 express the fact of the Incarnation, with its consequences for humanity: "His kindness has humbled His greatness*; He became like me, in order that I might receive Him"; and the next verse (6), "He was reckoned like myself, in order that I might put Him on" alludes to the putting on of Christ in baptism, of which St Paul speaks in Gal. iii 27, a verse recited thrice in the Mass of the Catechumens in the Liturgy of St Chrysostom†. Cp. Odes xi 10, xiii 2, xxxiii 10. We may cite also in illustration the phrases of a hymn prescribed to be sung by the deacons at the close of two baptismal *ordines* of the Syrian Church, printed by Assemani‡, as they bring out well the prominence given in these rites to the idea that the baptized are clad with the Lord's vesture:—" Descendite, fratres obsignati, induite Dominum nostrum et commiscemini inclyto ipsius generi, ut ait in sua parabola. De summo natura eius est; vestimentum vero ex imis. Mistum est vestimentum vestrum cum vestimento Domini nostri."

v. 11. Cp. Ode viii 16.

v. 12. "He pitied me in His grace." There is no direct allusion to sin or repentance in the Odes, a strange omission (see *Introd.* p. 22); but here it is said that man's state called forth the Divine Pity, which virtually implies the doctrine of the Fall. And so at the end of the verse, the Divine "sacrifice," sc. the Sacrifice of the Cross, is mentioned. Nestle (cited by Harris) has conjectured with much ingenuity that the text is here corrupt, and that for "sacrifice" we should read "essence," οὐσίας having been misread for θυσίας. But, apart from the fact that this would postulate a Greek original for the Odes (see *Introd.* p. 9), the sequence of thought demands *sacrifice* here, the Divine Pity being consummated in the Atonement of

---

* Cp. Phil. ii 6.
† Brightman, *Liturgies Eastern and Western*, p. 369.
‡ *Cod. Liturg.* II. 299. See Denzinger, *Rit. Orient.* I. 307.

ODES OF SOLOMON

Christ. And, on the other hand, as Grimme points out, the phrase "to receive of His *essence, because* He it is that is incorrupt and the fullness of the ages" would be inconsequent.

v. 14. God has sent Christ to be seen by men, that thus they may "know the Father.'

v. 15. Cp. Ps. c 3.

v. 17. "The footprints of His light." Connolly appositely compares Ode x 7 "the footprints of the light were set upon their heart," and points out that the thought in the two passages is the same, viz. that footprints are left on the road or in the hearts of believers to guide them in the way in which they should walk. Cf. Ode xxix 7 "He led me by His light."

v. 18. The Light created by God (Gen. i 3) rests in the Son; a characteristically Johannine thought. Harris has "He was resting in the Son," but the rendering I have adopted gives a clearer sense.

v. 24. So Clement says of the baptismal enlightenment: "Knowledge is the illumination we receive, which makes ignorance disappear*."

ODE VIII.

¹ Open ye, open ye your hearts to the exultation of the Lord: ² and let your love be multiplied from the heart and even to the lips, ³ to bring forth fruit to the Lord, a holy life†, and to talk with watchfulness in His light. ⁴ Rise up, and stand erect, ye who sometime were brought low: ⁵ tell forth, ye who were in silence, that your mouth hath been opened. ⁶ Ye therefore that were despised, be henceforth lifted up, because your righteousness hath been exalted. ⁷ For the right hand of the Lord is with you: and He is your helper: ⁸ and peace was prepared for you, before ever your war was. ⁹ Hear the word of truth, and receive the knowledge of the Most High. ¹⁰ Your flesh has not known what I am saying to you: neither have your hearts known what I am shewing to you. ¹¹ Keep my secret, ye who are kept by it: ¹² keep my faith, ye who are kept by it: ¹³ and understand my knowledge, ye who know me in truth. ¹⁴ Love me with affection, ye who love: ¹⁵ for I do not turn away my face from them that are mine; ¹⁶ for I know them, and before they came into being I took knowledge of them, and on their faces I set my seal: ¹⁷ I fashioned their members: my own breasts I prepared for them that they

---

* *Paed.* I. 6 (116 P). † So Ungnad and Stärk translate.

might drink my holy milk and live thereby. ¹⁸ I took pleasure in them and am not ashamed of them: ¹⁹ for my workmanship are they and the strength of my thoughts: ²⁰ who then shall rise up against my handiwork, or who is there that is not subject to them? ²¹ I willed and fashioned mind and heart: and they are mine, and by my own right hand I set my elect ones: ²² and my righteousness goeth before them and they shall not be deprived of my name, for it is with them. ²³ Ask, and abound, and abide in the love of the Lord, ²⁴ ⌐and⌐ ye beloved ones in the Beloved: those who are kept, in Him that liveth: ²⁵ and they that are saved in Him that was saved: ²⁶ and ye shall be found incorrupt in all ages to the name of your Father. Hallelujah.

The key to the understanding of this Ode, especially of its first half, is found in a Prayer for the Catechumens preserved by Chrysostom in his second homily on 2 Corinthians. I transcribe this Prayer from the Liturgy of Antioch as restored by Mr Brightman* from Chrysostom's writings, and place beside it vv. 1—13 of our Ode.

Ὑπὲρ τῶν κατηχουμένων ἐκτενῶς δεηθῶμεν
. . . . . .

Στῶμεν καλῶς· δεηθῶμεν
ἵνα ὁ παντελεήμων καὶ οἰκτίρμων θεὸς
ἐπακούσῃ τῶν δεήσεων αὐτῶν
ἵνα διανοίξῃ τὰ ὦτα τῶν καρδιῶν
αὐτῶν καὶ κατηχήσῃ αὐτοὺς τὸν
λόγον τῆς ἀληθείας
ἵνα κατασπείρῃ τὸν φόβον αὐτοῦ ἐν αὐτοῖς καὶ βεβαιώσῃ τὴν πίστιν
αὐτοῦ ἐν ταῖς διανοίαις αὐτῶν
ἵνα ἀποκαλύψῃ αὐτοὺς τὸ εὐαγγέλιον
τῆς δικαιοσύνης
ἵνα αὐτοῖς δῷ νοῦν ἔνθεον σωφρόνα
λογισμὸν καὶ ἐνάρετον πολιτείαν,
διαπαντὸς τὰ αὐτοῦ νοεῖν τὰ αὐτοῦ φρονεῖν . . . .

. . . . [ἐγείρεσθε]
τὸν ἄγγελον τῆς εἰρήνης αἰτήσατε
οἱ κατηχούμενοι

¹ Open ye, *open ye your hearts* to the exultation of the Lord: ² and let your love be multiplied from the heart and even to the lips, ³ to bring forth fruit to the Lord, a holy life, and to talk with watchfulness in His light. ⁴ *Rise up, and stand erect,* ye who sometimes were brought low: ⁵ tell forth, ye who were in silence, that your mouth hath been opened. ⁶ Ye therefore that were despised, be henceforth lifted up, because your *righteousness* hath been exalted. ⁷ For the right hand of the Lord is with you, and He is your helper: ⁸ and *peace was prepared for you,* before ever your war was. ⁹ Hear *the word of truth,* and receive *the knowledge of the Most*

---

* Brightman, *l.c.* p. 471.

εἰρηνικὰ ὑμῖν πάντα τὰ προκείμενα εἰρηνικὴν τὴν παροῦσαν
ἡμέραν καὶ πάσας τὰς ἡμέρας τῆς
ζωῆς ὑμῶν αἰτήσασθε

High. ¹⁰Your flesh has not known what I am saying to you; neither have your hearts known what I am shewing to you. ¹¹Keep my secret, ye who are kept by it: ¹²*Keep my faith*, ye who are kept by it: ¹³and *understand my knowledge*, ye who know me in truth.

The Liturgy of Antioch is, without doubt, much older than the days of Chrysostom, and it may well have been in existence in its main features in the second century. It is even possible that the parallels which have been indicated between the phrases of the Prayer for the Catechumens* and the words of our Odist shew that the writer of the Ode composed his poem with these phrases in his mind.

With the beginning of this Ode should be compared the beginning of Ode ix, "Open your ears and I will speak to you"; cp. also Ode xv 4, "Ears have become mine, and I have heard His truth." These phrases recall the fact that the ceremony of the *traditio* or delivery of the Gospel to the catechumens was called in the West "the Opening of the Ears†." So far as is known, this was a Western, not an Eastern, ceremony; but the petition "that He would open the ears of their hearts" occurs in the Prayer for the Catechumens just cited.

Chrysostom's commentary on this must now be transcribed‡: "'Ears' he saith, not those which be outward, but those of the understanding....For they have not heard the untold mysteries; but they stand somewhere at a distance, and far off from them; and even if they should hear of them, they know not what is said; for those [mysteries] need much understanding, not hearing only; and the inward ears as yet they have not; therefore also he next invoketh for them a prophet's gift, for the prophet spake on this wise 'God giveth me the tongue of instruction, that I should know how to speak a word in season'; for He openeth my mouth; 'He gave to me betimes in the morning; He granted me a hearing ear' (Isa. l 4)....Wherefore, he says, 'teach (κατηχήσῃ) them the word of truth,' so that it may echo back (ἐνηχεῖσθαι) from within them, for as yet they know not the word of truth as they ought to know....Whence also he adds 'And confirm his faith in their minds,' that is, that it may not lie on the surface, but strike its root deep downwards."

* We may also compare the similar Prayer for the Catechumens in the Syrian rite, as preserved in the *Apostolic Constitutions* (vIII. 6), and printed by Brightman (*l.c.* p. 4). But the parallels to our Odist are clearer in Chrysostom's Liturgy.

† Cp. Duchesne, *Christian Worship* (Engl. Tr.), p. 301, for a description of this ceremony, and see Brightman *l.c.* pp. 4, 471.

‡ *Hom.* II. *in 2 Cor.* § 7. See also the passage quoted above on Ode vi 14 from Chrysostom.

v. 3. "To bring forth fruit to the Lord." The continual exhortation of Christian teachers to the newly baptized was that they should "bring forth fruit," as it was the exhortation of the Baptist in the beginning*; and thus prayers for the neophytes that they may be fruitful in good works are frequent in the baptismal *ordines*. In the Epistle of Barnabas there is a typical passage†. The writer is recalling Old Testament foreshadowings of baptism, and he quotes Ps. i 1 ff. (of the tree planted by the waterside, which brings forth its fruit in due season), and Ezek. xlvii 1, 7, 12 (the passage that has already been before us when discussing Ode vi). His conclusion is τοῦτο λέγει ὅτι ἡμεῖς μὲν καταβαίνομεν εἰς τὸ ὕδωρ γέμοντες ἁμαρτιῶν καὶ ῥύπου, καὶ ἀναβαίνομεν καρποφοροῦντες ἐν τῇ καρδίᾳ, *i.e.* "we rise up from the waters of baptism bearing fruit in the heart." Or, as Cyril puts it, καρποφορήσωμεν τοίνυν ἀξίως‡. Let us place beside these passages the opening words of Ode xi: "My heart was circumcised and its fruit appeared; and grace sprang up in it; and *it brought forth fruit to the Lord.*" The idea appears in several other Odes; *e.g.* Ode xiv 7, "Teach me the Psalms of thy truth, that I may bring forth fruit in thee"; Ode xxxviii 18, "He set the root and watered it and fixed it and blessed it; and its fruits are for ever." When the patristic parallels are considered, they give good reason for concluding that the "fruit-bearing" in the Odist's thought is the "fruitbearing" which the baptized Christian is expected to exhibit.

For "living fruit" cp. Ephraim, "The tree of life will satisfy thee, and extend to thee its living fruits§."

"To talk with watchfulness in His light"; cp. Eph. v 9, ὁ καρπὸς τοῦ φωτός, and see on Ode xv 3.

v. 4. "Rise up, and stand erect, ye who sometime were brought low." The image is suggested by the posture of the catechumens during the Liturgical Prayer. The prayer begins: στῶμεν καλῶς; and the rubric prefixed is: οἱ κατηχούμενοι χάμαι κεῖνται καὶ ὁ διάκονος λέγει....Then towards the end the call is ἐγείρεσθε (see above, p. 63), when they stood up. Here this ceremonial is applied spiritually.

v. 5. "That your mouth hath been opened." Notice how close this is to Chrysostom's comment on the Prayer for the Catechumens. The "prophet's gift" is invoked for them, he says, by which he explains that he means "the tongue of instruction" mentioned in Isa. l 4; and then he inserts in the middle of his quotation the comment "for He openeth my mouth."

v. 7. "He is your helper"; cp. Odes vii 3, xxi 1, xxv 2.

v. 8. "Peace was prepared for you, before ever your war was." The catechumens were bidden to pray for εἰρηνικὰ ὑμῖν πάντα τὰ προκείμενα (see p. 63). Cp. Odes ix 6 and xxxv 2.

v. 9. "The word of truth." Here, again, we have a phrase from the Prayer for the Catechumens. Chrysostom explains their need of instruction:

---

* Matt. iii 8.   † § 11; see above, p. 57.   ‡ *Cat.* i. 4.
§ See Burgess, *The Repentance of Nineveh*, by Ephraim, p. 180.

"Teach them the word of truth...for as yet they know not the word of truth, as they ought to know." Our Odist proceeds (v. 10) in like manner: "Your flesh hath not known what I am saying to you; neither have your hearts known what I am shewing to you."

The idea of *truth* appears very frequently in the Odes. They are "Psalms of God's truth" (Ode xiv 7). See also Odes ix 8, xi 3, 4, xii 1, 11, 12, xvii 5, 7, xxv 10, xxxii 2, xxxiii 8 and especially Ode xxxviii 1, 4, 7, 10.

v. 10. Here there seems to be a change of personality. Vv. 1—9 are the utterance of the Church, from v. 10 to v. 22 the Speaker is God (see on v. 17), the Church taking up her counsel again at v. 23.

The Syriac text gives "neither has your *raiment* known, etc." If this is to stand, the "raiment" is the mortal body of man, the second clause of the verse being parallel to the first. But Dr Harris's emendation, which gives "hearts" for "raiment" is very attractive, and it has been widely adopted by scholars.

v. 11. "Keep my secret, ye who are kept by it." This seems to refer to the *disciplina arcani*, which was strictly observed*. Dr Harris cites a good parallel from Lactantius†, which undoubtedly has this reference: "nos defendere hanc (doctrinam) publice atque asserere non solemus, Deo iubente, ut quieti ac silentes arcanum eius in abdito atque intra nostram conscientiam teneamus...abscondi enim tegique mysterium quam fidelissime oportet, maxime a nobis, qui nomen fidei gerimus‡." In Cyril of Jerusalem, we have an even closer parallel to our Odist; it is his exhortation to the catechumens§, τήρησον τὸ μυστήριον (the exact words of Ode viii 11) τῷ μισθαποδότῃ.

If the words "Keep my secret" in the verse before us mean "Guard my secret from profane eyes," then the reference to the *disciplina arcani* is certain. But they *may* mean no more than "Do not lose my secret; keep it for your soul's health"; and in that case v. 11 is strictly parallel to v. 12, which—as we shall see—is an exhortation to catechumens.

v. 12. Once more our Odist reproduces the words of the Prayer for the Catechumens, and it will be observed that he takes up its phrases in their order, and in the order which Chrysostom follows when commenting on them. "Whence also he adds," says Chrysostom, "'And confirm his faith in their minds,' that is, that it may not lie on the surface, but strike its root deep downwards."

v. 13. See on Ode vi 5. Compare especially with vv. 4, 13 the following exhortation: "Rise up and put on the glory of baptism and receive the grace

---

* See *Introd.* p. 23.

† *Div. Inst.* iv. 12.

‡ Harris also cites a saying ascribed to Christ in Clem. Alex. *Strom.* v. 10, μυστήριον ἐμὸν ἐμοὶ καὶ τοῖς υἱοῖς μου, which goes back to a Hexaplar reading in Isa. xxiv. 16. But this parallel, although interesting, does not help towards the interpretation of our Ode.

§ *Procat.* 12.

of the Lord and assume perfection, and shine in excellence and not in precepts but in knowledge also*." The tone of this is exactly that of our Odes.

v. 16. Here is expressed God's foreknowledge of His people before they were born; cp. Ode vii 11.

For baptism as a seal, cp. Ode iv 8 and the note at that place. Mr Aytoun compares here the ninth century *Exposition of Baptism* by Moses bar Kepha: "He is sealed with *myron*...upon the organs of sense that they may not be the entrances of sin. Again on the forehead that he may be terrifying to demons....Again on the joints [members] that they may be the instruments of righteousness†."

v. 17. The breasts and milk of God are mentioned again, Ode xix 1—4; cp. Odes xiv 2, xxxv 6. Clement of Alexandria explains this for us in his *Paedagogus*‡. In the course of a long and intricate argument against the Gnostics, he brings together the passages 1 Cor. iii 2, γάλα ὑμᾶς ἐπότισα; 1 Pet. ii 2, ὡς βρέφη τὸ λογικὸν γάλα ἐπιποθήσατε; and Luke xi 27, 28. The Word is the true nutriment of the Christian soul. Like mother's milk, it is given to babes as soon as they are spiritually born, but it is never superseded by stronger food. It cannot be, for it is perfect nutriment; it is not essentially different from meat; it is the finer part of the blood, and Christ says that we must drink His blood. Scripture is, then, consistent with itself when it describes the perfect life as fed with milk and honey (Exod. iii 8). The Milk of the Word is for the newly baptized and for the perfect Christian alike. "If we have been regenerated into Christ, He who has regenerated us nourishes us with His own milk, the Word." And again: "As soon as we are regenerated, we are honoured by receiving the good news of the hope of rest, even the Jerusalem above, in which it is written that milk and honey fall in showers."

Now God supplies the milk in a mother's breast, and so too He supplies the Milk of the Word. We must seek "the care-dispelling breast of the Father," τὸν λαθικηδέα μαζὸν τοῦ πατρός; and "to those babes that seek the Word, the Father's breasts of love supply milk." That is, the Milk of the Word, for Clement, flows from the breasts of the *Father*, and is given to the baptized, just as our Odist conceives it.

So, too, a Poem on Easter, ascribed to the sixth century writer Fortunatus, speaks of the newly baptized as "fed with abundant milk at the Church's bosom." And Ephraim speaks of the soul's affections sucking the breast of wisdom §.

The equation, *Milk* = *Word*, meets us again in a different sequence of thought in Irenaeus‖: Christ came to earth in such manner as we could

---

* From *The Conflict of Severus of Antioch* by Athanasius, transl. from the Ethiopic by E. Goodspeed (*Patr. Orient.* iv. 6).

† *Expositor*, Oct. 1911, p. 341.   ‡ i. 6.

§ In a passage quoted by Morris (*Select Works of Ephraim*, p. 364 n.).

‖ *Haer.* iv. 38. 1, 2. I owe this reference to the kindness of Mr Edmund Bishop.

receive Him. He could have come in His glory, but we could not have borne it. "And on this account, as to babes, the *perfect bread* of the Father offered Himself to us as *milk* (i.e. His Advent as man), that we being nourished by the breast as it were of His flesh, and accustomed by this lactation to eat and drink the *Logos* of God, might be able to retain in ourselves the bread of immortality which is the *Spirit* of the Father."

The Description in the Egyptian Church Order* of the communion of the newly baptized introduces, as the General Editor points out to me, a similar (although not identical) idea, viz. the interpretation of *milk* as representing the *flesh* of Christ. Three cups are given to the neophytes: (1) water, accompanied by the words *in deo patre*, (2) milk and honey, (?) with the words, *et domino Jesu Christo*, and (3) wine, with the words *et spiritu sancto et sancta ecclesia*. The symbolism of these cups is interpreted thus: the wine is the symbol of the Blood of Christ; "lac et melle mixta simul ad plenitudinem promissionis quae ad patres fuit, qua[m] dixit terram fluentem lac et mel, qua[m] et dedit carnem suam Christus per quam sicut parvuli nutriuntur qui credunt in suavitate verbi amara cordis dulcia efficiens"; the water, "in indicium lavacri" &c.†

These passages shew that the representation of the Word as Milk, and the interpretation of Milk as the Flesh of the Word, were current in the second and third centuries. See further on Ode xix 2.

Similar thoughts, though not elaborated so fully, are expressed in the Syriac Homily of Narsai *On the Mysteries of the Church and of Baptism*: "As milk he sucks the Divine mysteries, and by degrees they lead him, as a child, to the things to come. A spiritual Mother [sc. the Church] prepares spiritual milk for his life; and instead of the breasts she puts into his mouth the Body and the Blood‡."

v. 18. Cp. Heb. ii 11, "He is not ashamed to call them breth en."

v. 21. "By my own right hand I set my elect ones." So Cyril charges the catechumens: "Be ye numbered among the holy and spiritual flock of Christ, to be set apart on His right hand"§; cp. Ode xix 5.

The title *electi* was reserved in the fourth century for those whose names had been registered and approved as candidates for baptism. In Jerusalem, in Cyril's day, this registration was made at the beginning of Lent: ὄνομα σου ἐνεγράφη‖. In the ninth century Moses bar Kepha mentions this

---

* Hauler, *Fragmenta Veronensia*, p. 112 f.; and cp. Achelis, *Texte u. Unters.* vi. 4. 100.

† We seem to have a reminiscence of this symbolic rite in Clement: "As is the union of the Word with baptism, so is the agreement of milk with *water*...and it is mixed with *honey* also, for cleansing along with sweet nutriment...furthermore, milk is mixed with sweet *wine*; and the mixture is beneficial, as when suffering is mixed in the cup in view of immortality." [*Paed.* i. 6 (127 P).]

‡ *Hom.* xxi. (C), p. 52, ed. Connolly.

§ *Cat.* i. 2.

‖ *Procat.* 4 and cp. *Cat.* iii. 3.

"enrolment" in connexion with baptism*. See further on Ode ix 12, and cp. Ode xxxiii 11.

v. 22. "They shall not be deprived of my name, for it is with them." Cp. Ode xviii 1, "that I might praise Him by means of my name." The baptized Christian receives a new name by which he is known also to God. For the virtue of the "Name," cp. Odes vi 6, xv 8, xxii 6, xxiii 20, xxv 11, xxxix 6, xli 17 and note that Cyril† applies to the baptismal name the LXX of Isa. lxv 15, 16: "Upon my servants shall a new name be called, which shall be blessed upon the earth." And, again, he tells the catechumens λαμβάνεις ὄνομα καινόν, ὃ πρότερον οὐκ εἶχες‡.

v. 23. Here the personality of the speaker changes again, and the Church concludes the Ode with words of holy counsel.

v. 25. The parallelism of *v.* 24 would lead us to expect "they that are saved in Him that saves," the Saviour; but we could only get this by correcting the manuscript text.

Ode IX.

¹Open your ears and I will speak to you. Give me your souls that I may also give you my soul, ²the word of the Lord and His good pleasures, the holy thought which He has devised concerning His Messiah. ³For in the will of the Lord is your life, and His thought is everlasting life; and your perfection is incorruptible. ⁴Be enriched in God the Father, and receive the thought of the Most High. ⁵Be strong, and be redeemed by His grace. ⁶For I announce to you peace, to you His saints; ⁷that none of those who hear may fall in war, and those again who have known Him may not perish, and that those who receive may not be ashamed. ⁸An everlasting crown for ever is Truth. Blessed are they who set it on their heads: ⁹a stone of great price is it; and there have been wars on account of the crown. ¹⁰And righteousness hath taken it and hath given it to you. ¹¹Put on the crown in the true covenant of the Lord. ¹²And all those who have conquered shall be written in His book. ¹³For their book is victory which is yours. And she (Victory) sees you before her and wills that you shall be saved. Hallelujah.

v. 1. "Open your ears." See on Ode viii 1 for this phrase. The baptized were anointed on the ears "that ye might receive ears quick to hear the divine mysteries§."

* Quoted by Aytoun, *Expositor*, Oct. 1911, p. 347.
† *Cat.* x. 16.   ‡ *Cat.* i. 4.   § Cyril, *Cat.* xxi. 4.

v. 2. For the Word as the Thought of God, cp. Ode xxviii 18 and xli 10, 11. In a prayer in the *Testamentum Domini** Christ is "the Thought of the Father"; and again † we have "We praise Thee, O Lord, who didst send thy Thought." See, further, p. 29 above.

v. 5. For the redemption of the baptized, see on Ode x 3; and for the grace of baptism see on Ode v 3.

v. 6. Cp. Ode viii 8.

v. 7. This warfare is the spiritual combat of the Christian; see p. 40.

vv. 8, 9. Truth is compared to a jewelled crown; those are blessed who wear it. In "the stone of great price" there may be a reference to "the white stone upon which there is a new name" of Rev. ii 17; this stone is interpreted in the Egyptian Church Order‡ of the course of instruction (including the knowledge of resurrection) before baptism. But the Apocalypse was not in the Syriac Canon, and there are no certain references to it in the Odes, so that this interpretation can hardly be pressed here. The image is quite intelligible without any such allusion; and the idea of truth being the precious crown of the baptized is suitable enough. For the allusions to the baptismal crown or chaplet in the Odes, see above on Ode i.

v. 12. As the Apocalypse was not in the Syriac Canon, the explanation of this "book" as the "book of life" of Rev. iii 5 is unlikely. It is more probable that the allusion is to the registration of the names of the catechumens; cp. Ode viii 21. A prayer for catechumens in a Coptic office runs: "scribe nomina eorum in libro tuo§." We may compare also the statement of Narsai that the priest "inscribes and writes body and soul [of the baptized] in the book of life||." We find in one of Ephraim's Epiphany Hymns: "To-day, lo! your offences are blotted out, and your names are written down. The priest blots out in the water, and Christ writes down in heaven¶." This last is not indeed a reference to any earthly registration but to the heavenly enrolment**, and so does not supply so exact a parallel to our Odist as Narsai's rhetorical statement. Yet the one was regarded as typical of the other, and so the illustration is worth giving.

Ode X.

¹The Lord hath directed my mouth by His word: and He hath opened my heart by His light: and He hath caused to dwell in me His deathless light; ²and gave me that I might speak the fruit of His peace: ³to convert the souls of them who are willing

---

* I. 26. † I. 32.

‡ § 46 (Tattam, p. 66); cp. also *Test. Domini*, II. 10.

§ Denzinger, *l.c.* I. 195.

|| *Hom.* XXII. B, p. 36 (ed. Connolly).

¶ *Epiphany Hymns*, VI. 13.

** Cp. Hebr. xii 23 and Hermas, *Vis.* I. 3 (with Gebhardt and Harnack's note).

ODE X

to come to Him: and to lead captive a good captivity for freedom.
⁴I was strengthened and made mighty and took the world captive;
⁵and it became to me for the praise of the Most High, and of God my Father. ⁶And the Gentiles were gathered together who were scattered abroad. ⁷And I was unpolluted by my love ⌜for them,⌝ because they confessed me in high places: and the footprints of the light were set upon their heart: ⁸and they walked in my life and were saved and became my people for ever and ever. Hallelujah.

In this Ode it would seem that Christ is the speaker throughout, and that its subject is the Mission of the Redeemer. Verse 1 would, indeed, apply more naturally to the disciple than to the Master, if it stood alone, but its words may perhaps be placed in the mouth of Christ, as the rest of the Ode must be.

v. 1. Cp. Ode xxxii 1, "light from Him that dwells in them."

vv. 3, 4. That in baptism Christ releases the captives who are bound is a familiar Christian thought. Baptism, says Cyril, is αἰχμαλώτοις λύτρον*, a phrase that is repeated often by the Fathers, *e.g.* by Gregory Nazianzen†; it is a ransom for captives, for those who are bound. So, in other Odes the singer speaks of this release. "I went over all my bondmen to loose them: that I might not leave any man bound" (Ode xvii 11); "He had cast off my bonds from me" (Ode xxi 1); "He who gave me authority over bonds that I might loose them" (Ode xxii 4); "I was rescued from my bonds" (Ode xxv 1). We may compare two phrases from Ephraim's hymns: "Blessed be He who has annulled the bonds‡," and "Bondmen in my baptism are set free§." See also Introduction, p. 34.

With the Ode generally we may compare part of a Hymn of Severus of Antioch: "He shewed everyone that He is He that was sent by the Father to proclaim and give release to the captives and to the blind the power of seeing the light, and to bestow upon us in His mercy a new regeneration through the laver of life-giving baptism ‖." Christ's Mission from the Father (*vv.* 1—3), His deliverance of captive souls (*v.* 4), His gift of light in baptism (*v.* 7) are all here.

v. 6. Cp. Ode xviii 7 "Thou wilt receive men from all quarters." The thought is of the universality of Christ's redemption which embraced both Gentile and Jew.

v. 7. "I was unpolluted by my love," sc. for the Gentiles. So Harris renders, and rightly¶. That it might be expected that union with the Gentiles would be a pollution is implied in a phrase of Aphrahat which it is

---

* *Procat.* 16. † *Oratio*, XL. 3.
‡ *Hymns on the Nativity*, xv. 9. § *Epiphany Hymns*, XIV. 38.
‖ *Patr. Orient.* VI. i. p. 77.
¶ He erases the plural points, so as not to read "by my sins."

apposite to quote here: "Joseph took to wife the daughter of the unclean priest, and Jesus espoused to Himself the Church taken from the unclean Gentiles*." The language of the Odist is thus quite compatible with a late second century date, although Harris thinks it implies the sentiments of the first century.

v. 7. "The footprints of the light were set upon their heart." See on Ode vii 17, and cp. the prayer in a Jacobite *Ordo baptismi*: "Largitor lucis...qui e tenebris lumen oriri fecisti : exorire in cordibus nostris†."

v. 8. "They...became my people," sc. the Gentiles, with whose redemption *vv.* 6—8 are concerned.

Ode XI.

¹My heart was circumcised and its flower appeared; and grace sprang up in it: and it brought forth fruit to the Lord, ²for the Most High circumcised me by His Holy Spirit and revealed my reins towards Him: and filled me with His love. ³And His circumcision of me became my salvation; and I ran in His way in His peace, even in the way of truth: ⁴from the beginning and even to the end I acquired His knowledge: ⁵and I was established upon the rock of truth, where He had set me up: ⁶and speaking waters touched my lips from the fountain of the Lord plenteously: ⁷and I drank and was inebriated with the living water that doth not die; ⁸and my inebriation was not one without knowledge, but I forsook vanity and turned to the Most High my God, ⁹and I was enriched by His bounty and I forsook the folly which is cast over the earth; and I stripped it off and cast it from me: ¹⁰and the Lord renewed me in His raiment, and possessed me by His light, and from above He gave me rest in incorruption; ¹¹and I became like the land which blossoms and rejoices in its fruits: ¹²and the Lord was like the sun shining on the face of the land; ¹³He lightened my eyes, and my face received the dew; and my nostrils‡ enjoyed the pleasant odour of the Lord; ¹⁴and He carried me to His Paradise; where is the abundance of the pleasure of the Lord; ¹⁵and I worshipped the Lord on account of His glory; and I said, Blessed, O Lord, are they who are planted in thy land! and those who have a place in thy Paradise; ¹⁶and they grow according to the growth of thy trees. And they have changed from darkness

* *Dem.* xxi. *Of Persecution*, § 9. † Denzinger, *l.c.* i. 271.
‡ Literally, "my breathing."

ODE XI

to light. ¹⁷Behold! all thy servants are fair, who do good works, and turn away from wickedness to the pleasantness that is thine: ¹⁸and they have turned back the bitterness of the trees from them, when they were planted in thy land; ¹⁹and everything became like a relic of thyself, and a memorial for ever of thy faithful works. ²⁰For there is abundant room in thy Paradise, and nothing is useless therein; ²¹but everything is filled with fruit; glory be to thee, O God, the delight of Paradise for ever. Hallelujah.

v. 1. "My heart was circumcised." That baptism is spiritual circumcision is a commonplace of early Christian writers. One parallel is enough, and it shall be from Cyril of Jerusalem*: ἁγίῳ πνεύματι διὰ τοῦ λουτροῦ περιτεμνόμενοι. These are the actual words of *v.* 2 "circumcised me by His Holy Spirit," except that the Odist suppresses, after his cryptic fashion, the technical term λουτρόν. For "grace" see on Ode v 3.

"Brought forth fruit." See above on Ode viii 3, for the connexion between baptism and fruit-bearing.

v. 3. "The way of truth"; see on Ode viii 9.

v. 4. For the acquisition of this divine knowledge see on Ode vi 5. Possibly Labourt is right in correcting the punctuation, so as to connect "from the beginning and even to the end" with *v.* 3 "I ran in His way...."

v. 6. With the "speaking waters" Harris compares Ignatius *Rom.* vii. ὕδωρ ζῶν καὶ λαλοῦν.

vv. 6, 7. See on Ode vi 10, 11 for the baptismal waters as a draught for the thirsty. The curious phrase "*inebriated* with the living water" is actually applied to the effects of the waters of baptism by Hilary. He expounds Ps. lxiv (lxv) 11, which runs in the Vulgate *Riuos eius inebria, multiplica genimina eius,* "We ourselves are thus inebriated when we receive the Holy Spirit who is called the River," and he proceeds to speak of the joy of the newly baptized.

v. 8. "My inebriation was not one without knowledge," in contrast with that described in Ode xxxviii 13.

v. 10. "The Lord renewed me in His raiment." See on Ode vii 6 and compare the striking phrase of Optatus, who calls Christ "tunica natans in aquis†."

A closer parallel may be found in a Hymn of the Baptized, found among the hymns of Severus of Antioch: "Ye that have been clad in the garment of salvation and the raiment of spiritual gladness by holy baptism, and have been adorned like a bride with the decoration and adornment of the Holy Spirit, keep the suprasensual beauty of comeliness that ye have received,

---

* *Cat.* v. 6; cp. Justin, *Tryph.* 43; Basil, *Hom.* xiii. *in baptismum* 2; and Chrysostom who expounds Col. ii 11 as relating to baptism.

† *De Schism. Donatist.* 5.

and the Lord will cause righteousness to sprout forth in you in a manner to be desired, like a bud or flower which springs from the earth*." The latter words recall v. 11, as the earlier recall v. 10. See on Ode xv 7—9.

v. 10. "He gave me rest in incorruption." See the note on Ode iii 6, for the significance of the allusions to *rest* in the Odes; and also see the note on v. 14 below.

v. 12. "The Lord was like the sun." So Gregory Nazianzen says in his Oration on Baptism†, "God is in the world of thought what the sun is in the world of sense."

v. 13. For the "dew" see on Ode iv 10.

"My nostrils enjoyed the pleasant odour of the Lord." Mr Aytoun quotes in illustration a statement of Moses bar Kepha that incense was burned before the baptized: "The incense that is burned before him shews this—the sweetness of the fragrance of the Father, Son, and Holy Ghost which he has received from baptism‡." But of this ceremony there is no early record, so far as I know; and an unsupported ninth century parallel can only be adduced with a *valeat quantum*. Yet it is significant that according to the *Exposition* of Moses, the burning of incense immediately preceded the entrance of the baptized to the "Holy of holies," which is likened to Paradise, a sequence which we find also here.

v. 14. "He carried me to His Paradise," with which compare "Come into His Paradise" (Ode xx 7). That the baptized had been, in a sense, restored to Paradise and its privileges, is a frequent thought with the Eastern Fathers. Origen expresses it clearly. Commenting on the words ἔθετο αὐτὸν ἐν τῷ παραδείσῳ§, he proceeds: οἱ ἀναγεννώμενοι διὰ τοῦ θείου βαπτίσματος ἐν τῷ παραδείσῳ τίθενται, τουτέστιν, ἐν τῇ ἐκκλησίᾳ ἐργάζεσθαι τὰ ἔνδον ὄντα ἔργα πνευματικά. So, too, in his Sermon on Christ's Baptism, Gregory of Nyssa exclaims: "The Jordan is glorified by regenerating men, and planting them in the Paradise of God; and of them, as the words of the Psalmist say, ever blooming and bearing the foliage of virtues 'the leaf shall not wither' and God shall be glad receiving their fruit in due season." Cyril has the same idea: "Then may the gate of Paradise be opened to every man and every woman among you‖"; "Henceforth thou art planted in the invisible (νοητόν) Paradise¶"; "There is opened to thee the Paradise of God**." In like manner, Paradise is described as the place of habitation of the baptized by Basil††, who asks: σὺ δὲ πῶς ἐπανέλθῃς εἰς τὸν παράδεισον, μὴ σφραγισθεὶς τῷ βαπτίσματι; Once again, in the Hymn of the Baptized already‡‡ quoted from Ephraim we have: "He opens for you His door, and bids you

---

* *Patr. Orient.* VI. i. p. 135.   † § 5.
‡ See *Expositor*, Oct. 1911, p. 343.   § *Sel. in Genesin.*
‖ Procat. 15.   ¶ *Cat.* I. 4.
** *Cat.* XIX. 9.
†† *Hom.* XIII. 2; this is a frequent topic with Cyril of Alexandria.
‡‡ See above, p. 20; and cp. the phrases of the hymn from the baptismal *Ordo* of Severus.

enter Eden (*v.* 10)...the fruit which Adam tasted not in Paradise, this day in your mouths has been placed" (*v.* 17). And a later writer, Moses bar Kepha, explains that "the entrance to the Holy of holies [after Baptism] signifies the entering into the tree of life from which Adam was prohibited*." It is in the same spirit, and surely with the same thoughts, that our Odist goes on with his song of joy: "He carried me to His Paradise, where is the abundance of the pleasure of the Lord; and I worshipped the Lord on account of His glory; and I said, Blessed, O Lord, are they who are planted in Thy land! and those who have a place in Thy Paradise, and they grow by the fruits of Thy trees...there is abundant room in Thy Paradise...I am altogether filled with fruit."

Dom Connolly† points out that we find in the *Apocalypse of Peter* a description of Paradise which recalls this Ode. The light (*v.* 12), the spaciousness (*v.* 20), the flowers (*v.* 11), the pleasant odours (*v.* 13), and the shining raiment (*v.* 10) are all in the *Apocalypse* as well as in our Ode.

v. 16. Compare the prayer for catechumens: "qui servos tuos a tenebris erroris ad agnitionem veritatis tuae vocasti‡."

v. 18. "The bitterness of the trees," sc. in contrast with the sweet fruits of the Paradise of the Church.

Ode XII.

¹He hath filled me with words of truth; that I may speak the same; ²and like the flow of waters flows truth from my mouth, and my lips shew forth His fruit. ³And He has caused His knowledge to abound in me, because the mouth of the Lord is the true Word, and the door of His light; ⁴and the Most High hath given it to His worlds, which are the interpreters of His own beauty, and the repeaters of His praise, and the confessors of His counsel, and the heralds of His thought, and the chasteners of His servants. ⁵For the swiftness of the Word cannot be expressed, and according to its swiftness so is its sharpness; ⁶and its course knows no limit. Never doth it fail, but it stands sure, and it knows not descent nor the way of it. ⁷For as its work is, so is its expectation: for it is light and the dawning of thought; ⁸and by it the worlds talk one to the other; and in the Word there were those that were silent; ⁹and from it came love and concord; and they spake one to the other whatever was theirs; and they were penetrated by the

---

* Quoted by Aytoun, *Expositor*, Oct. 1911, p. 341.
† *Journal of Theological Studies*, Jan. 1912, p. 302.
‡ Denzinger, *l.c.* I. 271 and *passim*.

Word; ¹⁰and they knew Him who made them, because they were in concord; for the mouth of the Most High spake to them; and His explanation ran by means of it; ¹¹for the dwelling place of the Word is man; and its truth is love. ¹²Blessed are they who by means thereof have understood everything, and have known the Lord in His truth. Hallelujah.

The doctrine of the Word contained in this Ode has already been examined*, and it has been shewn that while the phraseology suggests Gnostic parallels, there is nothing characteristically Gnostic involved. It is unnecessary to repeat here what has been said before; and therefore a very few notes will suffice.

v. 1. See on Ode viii 9 for "words of truth."

v. 2. See on Ode viii 3 for the "fruitbearing of the baptized"; and cp. Hebr. xiii 15.

v. 3. See on Ode vi 5 for the knowledge of God imparted to the catechumens. "The door of His light"; see on Ode xv 3.

v. 5. I have adopted Dr Barnes's rendering of this verse†. Cp. Hebr. iv 12, where "swiftness" and "sharpness" are, as here, characteristics of the energy of the Logos. This passage in Hebrews seems to have been in the writer's mind, for the adjective "sharp" as applied to the Word has no other Biblical authority. Dr Burkitt points out to me that the mention of "worlds" in *v.* 4 recalls Hebr. i 2.

v. 7. Cp. Ode xvi 16, and see above, p. 29. I adopt a rendering of this verse suggested to me by Dr Burkitt.

v. 11. Cp. Ephraim "that He might come and make us a dwelling-place for His sender‡." I cannot find, as Harris does, any distinction between the doctrine of our Odist and the Johannine doctrine of the Incarnation.

Ode XIII.

¹Behold, the Lord is our mirror: open the eyes and see them in Him: and learn the manner of your face: ²and tell forth praise to His spirit: and wipe off the filth from your face: and love His holiness, and clothe yourselves therewith: ³and be without stain at all times before Him. Hallelujah.

The Lord is like a mirror in which we see ourselves as we are, filthy and in need of cleansing. Ephraim has a similar thought: "Thy mirror is clear, and all of it turneth towards Thee. Thy brightness inciteth the filthy to cleanse themselves thereon, since no impurity can be joined unto Thee, unless

* *Introd.* p. 28.
† See *Expositor*, July 1910, p. 59.   ‡ *Hom.* I. 1 "On our Lord."

it hath wiped from it its stains*." And in another place he says: "The Gentiles praise Thee that thy Word has become a mirror before them, that in it they might see death secretly swallowing up their lives†."

So too in the Hymn in the *Acta Joannis*, Christ is represented as saying: "I am a mirror to thee who perceivest me‡."

In one of his hymns§ Ephraim compares the water of baptism to a mirror, but this thought is hardly explicit here if the text be rightly preserved. Yet the "putting away the filth of the flesh" (1 Pet. iii 21) and the "putting on" of Christ (Gal. iii 27) are baptismal ideas which are not far from the thought of the Odist. Compare with *v.* 2, Ode vii 6 and Ode xi 10.

Ode XIV.

¹As the eyes of a son to his father, so are my eyes, O Lord, at all times towards thee. ²For with thee are my breasts and my delight. ³Turn not away thy mercies from me, O Lord: and take not thy kindness from me. ⁴Stretch out to me, O Lord, at all times thy right hand: and be my guide, even unto the end, according to thy good pleasure. ⁵Let me be well-pleasing before thee, because of thy glory, and because of thy name: ⁶let me be preserved from evil, and let thy meekness, O Lord, abide with me, and the fruits of thy love. ⁷Teach me the Psalms of thy truth, that I may bring forth fruit in thee: ⁸and open to me the harp of thy Holy Spirit, that with all its notes I may praise thee, O Lord. ⁹And, according to the multitude of thy tender mercies, so thou shalt give to me; and hasten to grant our petitions; and thou art able for all our needs. Hallelujah.

This Ode resembles the canonical Psalms; it is spoken throughout *ex ore catechumeni*.

v. 2. For "breasts" see on Ode viii 17.

v. 4. Cp. the prayer in a Syrian baptismal office: "Tu, Domine, dexteram misericordiae tuae extende super hanc ancillam tuam∥."

v. 7. For the "fruitbearing" of the baptized, see on Ode viii 3.

v. 8. For "the harp of thy Holy Spirit," see on Ode vi 1.

---

* Rhythm, xii. 5 (ed. Morris, p. 154).   † *Hom.* i. 5 "On our Lord."

‡ *Apocrypha Anecdota*, ser. ii. ed. M. R. James, p. 12.

§ *Epiphany Hymns*, ix. 7. Cp. Moses bar Kepha, "When thou lookest in water thou seest in it another in thine own likeness like thee....Thou goest down to baptism one person and comest up another." (See *Expositor*, Oct. 1911, p. 344.)

∥ Denzinger, *l.c.* i. 290.

Ode XV.

¹As the sun is the joy to them that seek for its daybreak, so is my joy the Lord; ²because He is my Sun and His rays have made me rise up; and His light hath dispelled all darkness from my face. ³In Him I have acquired eyes and have seen His holy day; ⁴ears have become mine and I have heard His truth. ⁵The thought of knowledge hath been mine, and I have been delighted through Him. ⁶The way of error I have left, and have walked towards Him, and have received salvation from Him, without grudging. ⁷And according to His bounty He hath given to me, and according to His excellent beauty He hath made me. ⁸I have put on incorruption through His name: and have put off corruption by His grace. ⁹Death hath been destroyed before my face: and Sheol hath been abolished by my word: ¹⁰and there hath gone up deathless life in the Lord's land, ¹¹and it hath been made known to all His faithful ones, and hath been given without stint to all those that trust in Him. Hallelujah.

v. 1. It is possible that in the opening phrases of this Ode we have an allusion to the fact that the time of baptism was before daybreak on Easter Day; cp. Ode xviii. 6 "Let not the luminary be conquered by the darkness." Cyril of Jerusalem refers to this when he says: "May God at length shew you that night, that darkness which shines like the day" (τὸ σκότος τὸ ἡμεροφανές)*.

Mr Aytoun quotes in illustration a passage from the *Exposition of Baptism* of Moses bar Kepha, a ninth century Syrian writer†: "By turning to the East and confessing Christ he signifies that he is confessing that Christ is the Light...and that He is the Sun of Righteousness."

v. 3. The idea of baptism as an illumination of the soul goes back to Heb. vi. 4, and is a commonplace in early Christian literature. Baptism is a φωτισμός‡, and the baptized are φωτισθέντες, *illuminati*. The explanation of this given by Moses bar Kepha is quoted by Mr Aytoun§, and is instructive: "Baptism is named Illumination for two reasons, (1) Because from him who is baptized there is expelled the darkness of the ignorance of God and the darkness of sin, and he is illumined by the three lights which are the Father, Son, and Holy Ghost. (2) Because he is counted worthy of the light of the Kingdom of Heaven, &c. It is designated Regeneration,

---

* Procat. 15. † *Expositor*, October 1911, p. 342.
‡ Cp. Just. Mart. *Apol.* I. 61; Clem. Alex. *Paed.* I. 6 (113 P); Greg. Naz. *Oratio* XL. 4.
§ *l.c.* p. 339.

being likened to the first birth from a woman. The first birth is from a woman, but this is of the Holy Spirit."

See further Odes x 7, xxi 5, xxxii 1, xli 6, and especially xxxvi 3 (where the two ideas of Illumination and Spiritual Birth are linked together, as here); cp. also for the idea of "light," Odes vii 17, viii 3, xii 3, xxv 7, xl 6.

Some commentators have thought that the words "Awake thou that sleepest and arise from the dead, and Christ shall give thee light" (Eph. v 14), come from an ancient baptismal hymn. At any rate the thought is similar to that of our Odist, repeatedly expressed.

v. 4. "Ears have become mine." See on Ode vjii 1 *supra* p. 64.

v. 5. See on Ode vi 5.

vv. 7—9. Mr Aytoun adduces an apposite parallel, again from Moses bar Kepha*. "The white robes [sc. of baptism; see further on Ode xxi 2] are... because beforetime he was without form or beauty, and it is come to pass that he has acquired both form and adornment, and because after the resurrection he will receive a robe of immortality and incorruption." As our Odist does, Moses bar Kepha thinks of baptism as giving a new beauty to the neophyte, and of the baptismal robe as a "garment of incorruption." Cp. the passage quoted from the Hymns of Severus of Antioch on Ode xi 10.

v. 8. The spiritual garment was often called "the garment of incorruption." A prayer for the catechumens in the Apostolical Constitutions† asks that they may be worthy of τὸ ἔνδυμα τῆς ἀφθαρσίας. A similar phrase is found in Cyril of Jerusalem ‡, and in Gregory Nazianzen, the words of the latter being "If you see any one naked, clothe him, in honour of your own garment of incorruption, which is Christ, for as many as were baptized into Christ have put on Christ§." So, too, Basil writes that in baptism κατεπόθη τὸ θνητὸν ἐν τῷ τῆς ἀφθαρσίας ἐνδύματι. Cp. Ode xxi 4 and xxxiii 10; and note a similar expression in a baptismal hymn of Ephraim: "Ye too in the water, receive from Him the vesture that wastes not." For "grace" see on Ode v 3.

For the virtue of the Name, see on Ode viii 22.

v. 9. If we may read "His word" for "my word" here, as Harris suggests, the hymn is throughout *ex ore catechumeni*; otherwise we must suppose a transition of personality at this point, and the rest of the Ode to be placed in the mouth of Christ.

Language of this kind most naturally applies to the victory of Christ over Death in Hades (cp. Ode xxii 11 f. and Ode xxxiii 2 f.), but, as has been shewn above (p. 32 f.), there is a close correspondence between the baptismal gnosis and that of the Descent into Hell, and similar language is used of the victory in both cases. In any event, the Ode must be Christian.

---

* *l.c.* p. 340.

† viii. 6. See also Brightman, *l.c.* 315, 471.

‡ *Cat.* xv. 26. § *Oratio* xl. 31.

Ode XVI.

¹As the work of the husbandman is the ploughshare; and the work of the steersman is the traction* of the ship: ²so also my work is the Psalm of the Lord: my craft and my occupation are in His praises: ³because His love hath nourished my heart, and even to my lips His fruits He poured out. ⁴For my love is the Lord, and therefore I will sing unto Him: ⁵for I am made strong in His praise, and I have faith in Him. ⁶I will open my mouth, and His spirit will utter in me ⁷the glory of the Lord and His beauty; the work of His hands and the operation of His fingers: ⁸the multitude of His mercies and the strength of His word. ⁹For the word of the Lord searches out all things, both the invisible and that which reveals His thought; ¹⁰for the eye sees His works, and the ear hears His thought. ¹¹He spread out the earth and He settled the waters in the sea: ¹²He measured the heavens and fixed the stars: and He established the creation and set it up: ¹³and He rested from His works: ¹⁴and created things run in their courses, and do their works: ¹⁵and they know not how to stand and be idle; and His ⌐heavenly⌐ hosts are subject to His word. ¹⁶The treasure-chamber of the light is the sun, and the treasury of the darkness is the night: ¹⁷and He made the sun for the day that it may be bright, but night brings darkness over the face of the land; ¹⁸and their alternations one to the other speak the beauty of God: ¹⁹and there is nothing that is without the Lord; for He was before anything came into being: ²⁰and the worlds were made by His word, and by the thought of His heart. Glory and honour to His name. Hallelujah.

This Hymn is occupied with the praises of the Word, and the agency of the Word in creation and in nature.

v. 16 recalls Ps. xix 1—5, "The heavens declare the glory of God....Day unto day uttereth speech, and night unto night sheweth knowledge....In them hath he set a tabernacle for the sun, which is as a bridegroom coming out of his chamber." The alternations of night and day are like an interchange of voices proclaiming the glory of the Creator; cp. Ode xii 8 "By it [sc. the Word] the worlds talk one to the other." See above, p. 30.

* Schultess and Labourt correct the text so as to read "the work of the pilot is the management of the mast."

Harris calls attention to *vv.* 13, 14, "He rested from His works: and created things run in their courses, and do their works: and they know not how to stand and be idle," for which he provides an interesting parallel from Justin Martyr "You observe that the heavenly bodies do not idle nor keep sabbath*." And again, when our Odist says "His heavenly hosts are subject to His word," he implies that God controls the movements of the worlds on Sabbath days as well as on week days, which Justin says explicitly a little lower down†. The Syriac commentator Isho'dad, who wrote in the ninth century but whose interpretations preserve much older material, on John v 17‡ represents Christ as saying: "Do I allow the circuit of the sun, the blowing of the winds, the flowing of the rivers, the bridling of the seas, the descent of the rain, the bringing forth of fruits, the birth and growth of men together, and the energies of all living beings about everything? These things which are accomplished *by means of angels*, according to His will; and *these things are done* in the feasts and *on the Sabbaths* and at every hour." So Clement of Alexandria has: "God's resting is not, then, as some conceive, that God ceased from doing. For being good, if He should ever cease from doing good, then would He cease from being God....The resting is, therefore, the ordering that the order of created things should be preserved inviolate§." Hilary says the same thing: "Est ergo opus Dei sabbato? Est plane; nam nisi esset, caelum dilaberetur, lumen solis occideret, terra non staret, fructuum omnii in incrementa deficerent; vitae hominum interirent, si sabbati lege virtutum omnium constitutio otiaretur. Sed requies nulla est, et cursus idem est, ut sex diebus, ita et sabbato elementorum omnium continentur officia||." That our Odist's idea is not specifically Jewish (as Harnack suggests) is clear.

Ode XVII.

¹I was crowned by my God: my crown is living: ²and I was justified in my Lord: my incorruptible salvation is He. ³I have been delivered from vanity, and I am not a condemned [man]: ⁴my chains have been cut off by His hands: I received the face and the fashion of a new person: I have entered therein and have been saved; ⁵and the thought of truth led me on. And I walked after it and did not wander: ⁶and all that have seen me were amazed: and I was regarded by them as a strange person: ⁷and He who knew and brought me up is the Most High in all His perfection. And He glorified me by His kindness, and raised my thought to the height of truth. ⁸And from thence He gave me

* *Tryph.* 23.   † *Tryph.* 29.
‡ *Horae Semiticae*, no. v. p. 234 (ed. M. D. Gibson).
§ *Strom.* vi. 16. || *Tract. de titulo Ps. xci.* § 7.

the way of His footsteps and I opened the doors that were closed, ⁹and brake in pieces the bars of iron; but my iron melted and dissolved before me; ¹⁰nothing appeared closed to me: because I was the door of everything. ¹¹And I went over all my*bondmen to loose them; that I might not leave any man bound or binding: ¹²and I imparted my knowledge without grudging: and my prayer was in my love: ¹³and I sowed my fruit in hearts, and transformed them into myself: and they received my blessing and lived; ¹⁴and they were gathered to me and were saved; because they were to me as my own members and I was their Head. Glory to thee our head, the Lord Messiah. Hallelujah.

This Ode is full of the thought of the Redemption of the Baptized.

v. 1 alludes to the baptismal crown or chaplet (see on Ode i).

vv. 3, 4. The translation which I have adopted for these verses is substantially that of Flemming.

v. 4. "I received the face and fashion of a new person." Almost the same words are used by Moses bar Kepha: "Thou goest down to baptism one person, and comest up another instead, the new instead of the old†."

v. 5. "The thought of truth led me on, and I walked after it, and did not wander." Cp. Ode xxxviii 2, 4, "The Truth took me and led me...and suffered me not to wander, because it was the Truth." See also on Ode viii 9.

v. 6. "I was regarded by them as a strange person." Cp. Ode xli 8, "All those will be astonished that see me, for of another race am I." See on Ode xxxvi 3 for baptism as the new birth.

v. 8. The earlier part of this Ode is spoken in the name of the baptized Christian, but the later part must be in the Name of Christ, a return being made at the end, "Glory to thee, our head, the Lord Christ," to the original speaker. It has been pointed out in the Introduction (p. 32 f.), that similar language is used by the Fathers of the effects of baptism and of Christ's descent into Hades, so that it may not always be easy to determine to which of these topics allusion is made. Here, however, it seems probable that the dominant thought is that of the redemption of the baptized and their deliverance from bondage.

v. 8. "He gave me the way of His footsteps." If the allusion is to the way which Christ trod from Sheol for the dead to follow in, we should compare Ode xxii 7 b. See note there.

vv. 8—10. "I opened the doors that were closed and brake in pieces the bars of iron...nothing appeared closed to me...." In Isa. xlv 1—3 we have, "I will loose the loins of kings to open the doors before him, and the gates

---

* N has 'the' for 'my.'

† From the *Expositio*, § 16 (quoted by Aytoun, *Expositor*, Oct. 1911, p. 354).

shall not be shut....I will break in pieces the doors of brass and cut in sunder the bars of iron ; and I will give thee the treasures of darkness and hidden riches of secret places*," which is obviously behind our Odist's language. These words were originally spoken of Cyrus "the anointed," but they are applied by Lactantius explicitly to Christ, and in the same section of his work in which he quotes Ode xix†. And two centuries before Lactantius, this verse from Isaiah is quoted by Barnabas (in a passage already cited in the notes on Ode vi 7), as one of a number of O.T. *testimonia* to baptism. I have pointed out in the *Introduction*‡ that Isa. xlv 2, 3 (a reminiscence of Ps. cvii 15, 17) is also quoted in the *Descensus ad inferos* as prophetic of the Harrowing of Hell; but the application in the Ode before us is, primarily, to the victory of baptism.

v. 9. "My iron melted and dissolved before me." The idea that baptism is like a purifying fire is to be found elsewhere. Thus Narsai has : "His own handiwork He made a craftsman over His creation, that it should recast itself in the furnace of the waters and the heat of the Spirit"; and again "As in a furnace he recasts bodies in baptism, and as in a fire he consumes the weeds of mortality§." So too in a Syriac hymn printed by Assemani∥ the words occur : "...found the lost coin, the royal image encrusted with passions, and rusted through sin, and purged it and cleansed it in the furnace of Holy Baptism." And Cyril in his Catechetical Lectures¶ has a similar thought. He says that as the water of baptism encompasses the body, so does the Spirit pervade the soul : "If the fire passing in through the mass of the iron makes the whole of it fire, so that what was cold becomes burning and what was black is made bright—if fire which is a body thus penetrates and works without hindrance in iron which is also a body, why wonder that the Holy Ghost enters into the very inmost recesses of the soul." Certainly the words of our Ode "my iron melted and dissolved before me" immediately follow the Isaiah quotation "I brake in pieces the bonds of iron," which is spoken *ex ore Christi*, and the Odist may have only meant to amplify this ; but it is interesting to observe that the image of the melting of iron in a furnace is one which is used to illustrate the purification of baptism and the action of the Spirit.

It is not to be overlooked, however, that the same idea of the melting of iron is applied to the dissolving of the iron gates of Hades when Christ descended. Τὰς ἀλύτους ἀλύσεις ὡς κηρὸν διαλύσας is the phrase used of the Harrowing of Hell by Pseudo-Epiphanius, in a Homily for Easter Eve**.

* The LXX. representing the last words is θησαυροὺς ἀνοίξω σοι.
† *Div. Inst.* iv. 12; see p. 4. Isa. xlv. 2, 3 is applied to Christ by Tertullian also (*adv. Judaeos* vii.).
‡ *Supra*, p. 36.
§ *Hom.* xxii. (B) ed. Connolly, pp. 41, 48.
∥ *Cod. Lit.* ii. 273, 274.   ¶ *Cat.* xvii. 14.
** Migne, *P. G.* xliii. 456.

84   ODES OF SOLOMON

v. 10. "Nothing appeared closed to me: because I was the door of everything." So in the Harrowing of Hell, Hades is bidden to "lift up its gates"...πάρεστι γὰρ Χριστὸς ἡ οὐράνιος θύρα*.

A remarkable passage from Hermas on Christ as the Gate may be cited here†: "'The Rock and the Gate, what is it?' 'This Rock,' saith he, 'and Gate is the Son of God.' 'How, Sir,' say I, 'is the Rock ancient, but the Gate recent?' 'Listen,' saith he, 'and understand, foolish man. The Son of God is older than all His creation, so that He became the Father's adviser in His creation. Therefore also He is ancient.' 'But the Gate, why is it recent, Sir?' say I. 'Because,' saith he, 'He was made manifest in the last days of the consummation; therefore the Gate was made recent, that they which are to be saved may enter through it into the Kingdom of God.'"

Christ is the Door or Gate, through whom is entrance to His Kingdom, both for the living and the dead. Denzinger cites a Nestorian baptismal *Ordo* in which we have: "O vera porta, aperire ei qui periit...fac nos intrare in ovile tuum," the allusion being to John x 9.

v. 11. For baptism as a release from bonds, see on Ode x 3 above; and compare the sequence of thought, "I went over my bondmen to loose them ...I imparted my knowledge without grudging," with the phrase of Clement, when speaking of baptism: "What ignorance has bound ill, is by knowledge loosed well; these bonds are as quickly as possible slackened by human faith and divine grace‡." Cp. *Introd.* p. 34.

v. 13. For the fruits of the Christian life see on Ode viii 3.

"I transformed them into myself." This is the exalted strain in which the singer speaks of the gift of baptism.

v. 14. "They were gathered to me." See on Ode xlii 19. "They were to me as my own members and I was their Head." See on Ode iii 2.

Ephraim § expresses himself in almost identical words:

> "Children of the Spirit ye have thus become;
> Christ has become for you the Head;
> Ye also have become His members."

Ode XVIII.

¹My heart was lifted up in the love of the Most High and was enlarged: that I might praise Him by means of my name. ²My members were strengthened that they might not fall from His strength. ³Sicknesses removed from my body, and it stood to the Lord by His will. For His kingdom is true. ⁴O Lord, for the sake of them that are deficient do not remove thy word from me!

---

* *Pseudo-Epiph. l.c.*
† Sim. ix. 12. See Odes xxii 12 and xxviii 15.
‡ *Paed.* i. 6 (116 P).   § *Epiphany Hymns*, ix. 1.

⁵Neither for the sake of their works do thou restrain from me thy perfection! ⁶Let not the luminary be conquered by the darkness; nor let truth flee away from falsehood. ⁷Thou wilt appoint me to victory; our salvation is thy right hand. And thou wilt receive men from all quarters, ⁸and thou wilt preserve from me all that hold fast by evil things*: ⁹Thou art my God. Falsehood and death are not in thy mouth: ¹⁰for thy will is perfection; and vanity thou knowest not, ¹¹nor does it know thee. ¹²And error thou knowest not, ¹³neither does it know thee. ¹⁴And ignorance appeared like chaff, and like the foam of the sea; ¹⁵and they supposed of that vain thing that it was something great; ¹⁶and they too came in likeness of it and became vain; and those have understood who have known and meditated; ¹⁷and they have not been corrupt in their imagination; for such were in the mind of the Lord; ¹⁸and they mocked at them that were walking in error; ¹⁹and they spake truth from the inspiration which the Most High breathed into them; Praise and great comeliness to His name. Hallelujah.

v. 1. "That I might praise Him by means of my name." This is the literal rendering of the Syriac, and the reference is to the new name which the Christian receives in baptism. See on Ode viii 22 for the virtue of the Name.

vv. 2, 3. For the supposed effects of baptism on the body, see on Ode vi 14.

v. 4. The "deficient in wisdom" are mentioned again in Ode xxiv 9.

v. 6. See on Ode xv 1.

v. 7. "Thou wilt receive men from all quarters"; cp. Ode x 6 for the catholicity of the outlook. We may compare a phrase from a Syriac Hymn on the Cross, found among the Hymns of Severus of Antioch: "Thou art in all things and hast filled all quarters†."

v. 14. "Chaff." So Schultess, and approved by Harris. The MSS. have "like a blind man."

Ode XIX.

¹A cup of milk was offered to me: and I drank it in the sweetness of the delight of the Lord. ²The Son is the cup, and He who was milked is the Father: ³and the Holy Spirit milked Him: because His breasts were full, and it did not seem good to

---

* So Burkitt, by a slight emendation of the text.
† *Patr. Orient.* vi. i. p. 117.

Him that His milk should be spilt for nought; ⁴and the Holy Spirit opened her bosom and mingled the milk from the two breasts of the Father; and gave the mixture to the world without its knowing it. ⁵And they who receive (it) are in the perfection of the right hand*. ⁶The womb of the Virgin caught (it), and received conception, and brought forth; and the Virgin became a Mother with many mercies; ⁷and she travailed and brought forth a Son, without incurring pain. ⁸Because it happened not emptily, and she had not sought a midwife (for He brought her to bear), she brought forth, as it were a man, by the will ⌐of God⌐; ⁹and she brought Him forth openly, and acquired Him in great power, ¹⁰and loved Him in salvation, and guarded Him in kindness, and showed Him in majesty. Hallelujah.

This Ode seems to fall into two divisions, each of five verses, and previous editors have failed to find any connexion between its parts. I would suggest that the key is to be found in the thought, already before us in Ode viii 17 (see note there), that the Milk of the Father is the Word, which is the spiritual food of the baptized Christian. The idea in our Odist is similar to that which we have already found in Clement and in Irenaeus, viz. that the Incarnation is a 'milking' of the Father, and that what was brought forth from the Virgin's womb is as milk received by the faithful†. This statement occupies *vv.* 1—5, and then we pass to the Coming of the Word, in the miraculous birth of Christ (*vv.* 6—10). Even thus interpreted, the Ode presents many difficulties; but it seems to be coherent on this hypothesis, as on no other.

v. 2. We have already seen (Ode viii 17) that to our Odist, as to Clement of Alexandria, the Word is the Milk flowing from the Breasts of the Father. Here the metaphor is elaborated further, and indeed confused, for the Son is the Cup.

v. 3. I have adopted Flemming's translation here: Harris has "it was necessary for Him that His milk should be sufficiently released," which is not easy to interpret. As I understand our Odist, he means that the Incarnation prevented, as it were, any waste of the Divine bounty.

v. 4. The Holy Spirit is spoken of as feminine in Syriac literature; see on Ode xxxvi 3.

---

* *vv.* 4, 5 are rendered thus by Connolly, whom I follow here.

† I have had the advantage of reading some notes by the general editor and Mr Edmund Bishop which deal with this interesting point. It seems probable that an idea was current in early speculation as to some connexion between Milk and the Incarnation. See on Ode viii 17.

"Without its knowing it." For the Word "was in the world and the world was made by Him and the world knew Him not" (John i 10). This is a Johannine thought.

v. 5. On the other hand, the Church of the baptized receive the Word. These are they "on the right hand": cp. Ode viii 21.

v. 6 is quoted by Lactantius* in the form: "Salomon ita dicit: *Infirmatus* est uterus virginis et accepit fetum et gravata est, et facta est in multa miseratione mater virgo." Harris suggests that *infirmatus* is in error for *insinuatus*; another suggestion is that of S. Reinach, who thinks that ἐθρύφθη was the Greek, θρύπτειν admitting equally of the renderings *perrumpere* and *insinuare*†. This assumes that the Odes were originally composed in Greek. Labourt translates "L'Esprit *étendit ses ailes* sur le sien de la Vierge." Flemming has "Er umarmte (?) den Leib der Jungfrau." Connolly supposes that the underlying Greek was ἐκράτησεν, Lactantius' *infirmatus est* being due to the corruption ἠκράτησεν. The original word must remain uncertain, but the tenor of the verse is not doubtful.

"The Virgin became a Mother with many mercies." The title *Mater misericordiae* naturally suggests itself, but this involves doctrinal thoughts later in origin than the second century. Batiffol suggests very plausibly that κεχαριτωμένη of Luke i 28 lies behind the Odist's words.

The collocation μήτηρ παρθένος is familiar in later theology, but it challenges attention here. (See on Ode xxxiii 5, for a passage in Clement of Alexandria where it is used of the Church.)

v. 7. "Without incurring pain." All these apocryphal details of a miraculous birth (as well as a miraculous conception) were current in the second century; *e.g.* in the *Ascension of Isaiah* xi 14 and the *Protevangelium* xix., xx. The painlessness of the birth was interpreted at a later date as being in contrast to Eve's childbearing. Cp. Epiphanius: ἀνεπαισχύντως, ἀχράντως, ἀμολύντως‡. Ephraim§ has the same: "the pure Virgin suffered not."

v. 8. I have followed Connolly's translation, although with hesitation. He suggests that 'emptily' represents the Greek κενῶς, which in its turn is a corruption of κοινῶς, so that the verse originally ran: "because it happened not in the common way." The notion that a midwife's services were not needed belongs to the early apocryphal literature of the Gospels, as above.

"He brought her to bear," sc. God, the aid of a midwife not being required. This was a patristic interpretation of Ps. xxii 9, "Thou art He that took me out of my mother's womb."

More literally, the latter part of this verse might be rendered, "She brought forth, as if she were a man, of her own will"; but I have followed Harris in adopting Batiffol's suggestion that the text means that the Virgin

* *Div. Inst.* iv. 12; see also *Epit. Div. Inst.* 44, and cp. *Introd.* p. 4.
† *Revue moderniste*, 1910, p. 458, cited by Labourt.
‡ *Anaceph.* p. 1136.
§ Rhythm iv. 1 (ed. Morris, p. 115).

brought forth Christ just as if He were *merely* man. She was really θεοτόκος, *Deipara*, to use the formula of a later time. Yet the text is quite orthodox; even Ephraim can say, "He was God in entering [the womb] and He was man in issuing*." Cp. Ode xxviii 14.

"By the will," sc. of God; He was born "not of the will of man, but of God." So the Old Latin of John i 13 quoted by Irenaeus† is "non enim ex voluntate carnis, neque ex voluntate viri, sed ex voluntate dei, verbum caro factum est."

v. 9. "She brought Him forth *openly*." Labourt renders the last word *en exemple*, and Batiffol ingeniously supposes it to represent the Greek ἐν ὁμοιώματι, as if the Childbearing of Mary were, in a sense, the ideal of maternity, dignified and painless. This is not convincing to me, but I can suggest nothing better.

v. 9. "Acquired Him in great power." Perhaps the thought is that of the Latin hymn‡ :

> Potestate, non natura
> fit creator creatura,

which Mone illustrates by Augustine's words "Christus natus non est per conditionem, sed per potestatem §," the "power" being the power of God. Batiffol compares Justin, *Tryph.* 54 : οὐκ ἐξ ἀνθρώπου σπέρματος, ἀλλ' ἐκ τῆς τοῦ θεοῦ δυνάμεως.

v. 10. "Loved Him in salvation." So the Syriac, which Harris emends so as to render "loved Him in His swaddling clothes," an attractive reading, but (as Flemming points out) one which destroys the parallelism of the last six clauses of the Ode. Perhaps "loved Him *in salvation*" is a reminiscence of the *Magnificat* "rejoiced in God *my Saviour*."

Batiffol attempts a restoration of the last six clauses in Greek, which at any rate brings out the rhythmical structure, like that of 1 Tim. iii 16.

> ὡς ἄνθρωπον ἐγέννησεν ἐκ θελήματος,
> ἐγέννησεν ἐν ὁμοιώματι,
> ἐκτήσατο ἐν δυνάμει,
> ἠγάπησεν ἐν σωτηρίᾳ,
> ἐφύλαξεν ἐν εὐφροσύνῃ,
> ἐφανέρωσεν ἐν μεγαλειότητι.

But there is nothing of Docetism in this, as Batiffol thinks; it is all quite orthodox.

See, for the conjunction of the Virgin Birth with the Harrowing of Hell, the passage cited in the *Introduction*, p. 39.

---

* *Hymns on the Nativity*, xiv.
† *Adv. Haer.* III. xvi. 2; cp. Tertullian, *de carne Christi*, 24.
‡ Mone, *Hymni Latini*, II. 85.   § *De Trin.* III. 26.

Ode XX.

¹I am a priest of the Lord, and to Him I do priestly service: and to Him I offer the sacrifice of His thought. ²For His thought is not like ⌜the thought of⌝ the world, nor ⌜the thought of⌝ the flesh, nor like them that serve carnally. ³The sacrifice of the Lord is righteousness, and purity of heart and lips. ⁴Present thy reins before Him blamelessly: and let not thy heart do violence to [another's] heart, nor thy soul to [another's] soul. ⁵Thou shalt not acquire a stranger by the blood of thy soul, neither shalt thou seek to deceive thy neighbour, ⁶neither shalt thou deprive him of the covering of his nakedness. ⁷But put on the grace of the Lord without stint; and come into His Paradise, and make thee a garland from its tree, ⁸and put it on thy head and be glad; and recline on His rest, and glory shall go before thee, ⁹and thou shalt receive of His kindness and of His grace; and thou shalt be flourishing in truth in the praise of His holiness. Praise and honour be to His name. Hallelujah.

v. 1. "Priestly service." That the service of the baptized is a priestly service is explicitly said by Chrysostom: "So also art thou thyself made king and priest and prophet in the Laver...a priest in that thou offerest thyself to God*." Cyril in like manner says he will remind the newly baptized that "like priests they have become partakers of the Name of Christ†." Burkitt, however, thinks that here and at Ode xxi 4 the Christian Eucharist is in view. See *Introd.* p. 23.

v. 3. The sacrifice which the baptized are to offer is that of justice and purity.

vv. 5, 6. These ethical precepts are of the kind in which catechumens were instructed. Moral teaching was always associated with the doctrinal or dogmatic teaching which preceded baptism. The prohibition against depriving a neighbour of "the covering of his nakedness" recalls Exod. xxii 26, 27, but there is no definite quotation.

Harris emends the Syriac of *v.* 5 so as to yield the translation, "Thou shalt not acquire a stranger by the price of thy silver." If this were the meaning, we should have here a prohibition of the practice of buying slaves, although neither Christianity nor Judaism condemned this as early as the second century. Slavery was not at first reckoned to be inconsistent with the Christian Gospel, any more than it was inconsistent with the Hebrew Law. The literal rendering of the Syriac gives a quite good sense: "Thou

---

* *Hom.* III. *in* 2 *Cor.*, sub fin.   † *Cat.* XVIII. 33.

shalt not acquire a stranger by the blood of (i.e. at the price of) thy soul." That is, the forcible capture of slaves by the sword was forbidden. *v. 5a* is really the continuation of *v. 4b*; crimes of violence are condemned.

Similarly *v. 6* is the continuation of *v. 5b*, both clauses meaning "Thou shalt be kind to thy neighbour, even beyond the demands of strict justice."

v. 7. For "the grace of the Lord" which is "put on" in baptism, see on Ode v 3.

For the idea that baptism restores man to Paradise, see on Ode xi 14.

For the baptismal garland, see on Ode i. Cp. Isa. xxxv 10.

v. 8. For the "rest of the Lord" see on Ode iii 6; and with the phrase "recline on His rest," cp. Ode xxxvi 1, "I rested on the Spirit of the Lord."

Ode XXI.

¹My arms I lifted up on high, even to the grace of the Lord: because He had cast off my bonds from me: and my Helper had lifted me up to His grace and to His salvation: ²and I put off darkness and clothed myself with light, ³and my soul acquired a body [*lit.* members] free from sorrow or affliction or pains. ⁴And increasingly helpful to me was the thought of the Lord, and His fellowship in incorruption: ⁵and I was lifted up in His light; and I served before Him, ⁶and I became near to Him, praising and confessing Him; ⁷my heart ran over and was found in my mouth: and it arose upon my lips; and the exultation of the Lord increased on my face, and His praise likewise. Hallelujah.

v. 1. The first act of the baptismal ritual was the renunciation of the devil; and then the catechumens with outstretched and uplifted hands faced eastward and professed their covenant with Christ. Cyril of Jerusalem describes this explicitly*, and we find the same thing in a rubric in the *Rituale Armenorum*†, where the priest "turns the catechumen to the east, and bids him raise his eyes to heaven, and *stretch out his hands*, confessing the Trinity." Tertullian speaks of this outstretching of the hands *after* baptism: "Cum de illo sanctissimo lavacro novi natalis ascenditis et primas manus apud matrem cum fratribus aperitis‡." A later witness, Moses bar Kepha, thus explains the significance of the act: "By spreading out his hands he declares that right willingly he confesses what he confesses and promises to do what he promises§." We have similar allusions in Odes xxvii 1, xxxv 8, xxxvii 1, xlii 1; see further on Ode xxvii 1.

* *Cat.* xix. 2; cp. Jerome *in Amos* vi. 14.
† Ed. Conybeare, p. 92.   ‡ *De Bapt.* 20.
§ Quoted by Aytoun, *Expositor*, Oct. 1911, p. 342.

Dr Plooij has worked out thoroughly the significance of this Extension of the Hands, which he has shewn to be a characteristically baptismal rite, widely spread in the East. It is not merely an attitude of prayer, but a distinct ceremonial act, prescribed sometimes where no prayer was said*.

"He had cast off my bonds from me." See on Ode x 3; 4 for baptism as a release from the bonds of sin, and compare the words of Moses bar Kepha†: "The divestiture of the baptized shews that he is delivered from the captivity, from the Adversary, like those who escape from captivity naked."

v. 2. "I put off darkness and clothed myself with light." The newly baptized were clothed in white robes, as we are informed by Cyril of Jerusalem. ἐνδυσάμενος τὰ πνευματικῶς λευκὰ are his words‡. He calls them "robes of light," ἔνδυμα φωτεινόν §, as Basil does too‖. Ephraim has the same thing: "Your vesture is shining and goodly your crowns¶." Moses bar Kepha explains the symbolism, after his manner**: "The white robes with which they clothe him are to shew that he has been in the darkness of ignorance and has become white and shining in the knowledge of God and in the light which he has received from baptism." Cp. Rom. xiii 12.

The baptismal alb is often spoken of by writers subsequent to the fourth century both in East and West. The Western Paschal hymn

> Ad coenam Agni providi
> et stolis albis candidi

is familiar. But early allusions to the baptismal robe are rare. It is possible, though not certain, that Tertullian alludes to it in the words: "Recuperabit et apostata vestem priorem, indumentum Spiritus sancti, et anulum denuo, signaculum lavacri††." There is a clear reference to it in the *Martyrium Matthaei* (c. 27), which may be of the third century. And perhaps a rubric in the *Testamentum Domini* may carry an allusion to the communion of neophytes: "Episcopus ante oblationem sacrificii congruenter dicat dicenda ad oblationem, *cum alba induti* ab invicem suscipientes dicant Alleluia‡‡." But it would seem that we have in the Ode before us the earliest clear allusion to the habit of clothing the neophytes in white robes, which afterwards became general§§. Cp. Ode xxv 7 "In me there is nothing that is not light," and see note on Ode xv 3.

v. 3. See on Ode vi 14 for the supposed beneficial influence of baptism upon the health of the body.

v. 4. For the garment of incorruption see on Ode xv 8.

---

* *De "Oranten"-houding in de Oden van Salomo* (Theologisch Tijdschrift, 1911, s. 449), an essay translated with additions in the *Expository Times* for Feb. and March 1912.

† *l.c.* p. 341. ‡ *Cat.* xxii. 9.
§ *Procat.* 16. ‖ *Hom.* xiii. *in bapt.* 5.
¶ *Epiphany Hymns*, xiii. 5. ** *l.c.* p. 340.
†† *De Pudicitia*, 9. ‡‡ ii. 12.

§§ See on the whole subject the article *Aubes baptismales* in Cabrol's *Dict. d'Archéologie Chrétienne.*

Ode XXII.

¹He who brought me down from on high also brought me up from the regions below; ²and He who gathers together the things that are betwixt is He also who cast me down*. ³He who scattered my enemies and my adversaries: ⁴He who gave me authority over bonds that I might loose them; ⁵He that overthrew by my hands the dragon with seven heads: and thou hast set me over his roots that I might destroy his seed: ⁶Thou wast there and didst help me, and in every place thy name was a rampart† to me. ⁷Thy right hand has destroyed his wicked poison‡; and thy hand has levelled the way for those who believe in thee: ⁸and thou didst choose them from the graves and didst separate them from the dead. ⁹Thou didst take dead bones and didst cover them with bodies; ¹⁰they were motionless, and thou didst give (them) energy for life. ¹¹Thy way was without corruption, and thy face; thou didst bring thy world to corruption: that everything might be dissolved, and then renewed, ¹²and that the foundation for everything might be thy Rock§: and on it thou didst build thy Kingdom; and it became the dwelling place of the saints. Hallelujah.

This is one of the Odes which are quoted in *Pistis Sophia*, and some of the Coptic renderings do not agree with the Syriac. The Ode deals with Christ's Descent into Hades and the consequences of His victory, but the connexion of thought is not clear at every point. The speaker is not the same throughout. Verses 1—6 are *ex ore Christi*, but the remaining verses express adoration and thankfulness on the part of the redeemed soul.

We may first place beside the opening verses some clauses descriptive of Christ's Victory in Hades, which are like the phrases of our Odist. They are from a Discourse by Hippolytus, of which only fragments are extant||, "Upon the Great Ode" (εἰς τὴν ᾠδὴν τὴν μεγάλην). It is not known what the "Great Ode" was—Ps. cxix and the Song of Moses have been suggested, though neither suggestion is probable—but it clearly was a Christian Hymn of Praise

---

* The Coptic has: "He who removed those who were in the midst has taught me concerning them."

† So N.

‡ The Coptic has: "the poison of the slanderer," sc. διάβολος.

§ The Coptic has "thy light."

|| Printed in Theodoret's Works, Vol. IV. p. 88 (ed. Sirmond); also in the Berlin edition of Hippolytus, Vol. I. pt II. p. 83.

similar to our Ode xxii. I have printed the clauses of Hippolytus' Discourse in separate lines for the better elucidation of the sense.

Ὁ τὸν ἀπολωλότα ἐκ γῆς πρωτόπλαστον ἄνθρωπον,
καὶ ἐν δεσμοῖς θανάτου κρατούμενον,
ἐξ ᾄδου κατωτάτου ἑλκύσας·
ὁ ἄνωθεν κατελθὼν
καὶ τὸν κάτω εἰς τὰ ἄνω ἀνενέγκας·
ὁ τῶν νεκρῶν εὐαγγελιστής,
καὶ τῶν ψυχῶν λυτρωτής,
καὶ ἀνάστασις τῶν τεθαμμένων γινόμενος
. . . . . .
ὁ οὐράνιος τὸν ἐπίγειον εἰς τὰ ἄνω καλῶν
. . . . . .
ὁ τὸν εἰς γῆν λυόμενον ἄνθρωπον,
καὶ βρῶμα ὄφεως γεγενημένον,
εἰς ἀδάμαντα τρέψας . . .

The topics are the rescue of Adam from Hades (cp. *v.* 1) and his release from bonds (cp. *v.* 4) by Him that came down from above (cp. *v.* 1); the resurrection of those that were dead and buried (cp. *v.* 8 f.); and the strengthening of man who had become dust—the serpent's meat.

That *v.* 1 must apply to Christ and not to the redeemed Christian seems certain. In the Discourse *On the Theophany** Hippolytus represents John Baptist as expressing his inferiority to Christ by saying: "I was brought up from beneath; I did not come down from above." Only One can be described as "He that cometh from above" (John iii 31), that is, Christ. In the opening verses of the Ode, then, the agent is God who gave power and authority to Christ whom He sent, and whom He brought back victorious from Hades. Yet it must be borne in mind (see *Introd.* p. 35) that the experiences of Christ in Hades were regarded as repeated, on a lesser scale, in the experience of every baptized person; so that what is said of Him might also, in a true sense, be said of His disciples. Thus Hippolytus, a little lower down in the same discourse†, describes the benefits of Christ's baptism: "How many blessings should we have lost, had the Lord yielded to John's entreaty and declined baptism! For the heavens were shut before this; the region above was inaccessible. We should in that case descend to the lower parts, but we should not ascend to the upper. But was it only that the Lord was baptized? He also renewed the old man, and committed to him again the sceptre of adoption. For straightway *the heavens were opened to Him*. A reconciliation took place of the visible with the invisible; the celestial orders were filled with joy; the diseases of earth were healed; secret things were made known; those at enmity were restored to amity."

The primary thought in our Ode is, however, the Victory of Christ in Hades. As Ephraim puts it: "This is He who descended to Sheol and ascended, that from [the place] which corrupts its sojourners, He might bring

7 *   * § 3.   † *Theoph.* 3.

us to the place which nourishes with its blessings its inhabitants...Sheol brought Him forth that through Him its treasures might be emptied out*." Or, as he has it in another place: "To thee be glory who didst descend and plunge after Adam, and drew him out of the depths of Sheol, and brought him into Eden†." So too the Prayer of Initiation in the *Testamentum Domini* ‡ invokes Christ as He "who in His soul descended in the Godhead to Sheol, who descended from the pure heights above the heavens."

v. 2 is obscure, and there is no certainty as to the text. In any case, the gathering together of the things between heaven and the lower regions seems to recall the creative act of Gen. i 9, when the waters under the heaven were "gathered into one place." This verse was much in the thoughts of the compilers of the baptismal liturgies§. "Qui in unum locum aquas congregasti" is a phrase in a baptismal prayer found in many Eastern rites‖. Thus a prayer in a Maronite service book begins: κύριε...ὁ συνάγων τὰ ὕδατα εἰς τὰς συναγωγὰς αὐτῶν¶. The meaning of the verse before us, then, seems to be that God, who in creation gathered together the waters and still coerces them in the mystery of baptism, is He who sent Christ the Redeemer to earth.

v. 3. Cp. Ps. lxvii (lxviii) 1: ἀναστήτω ὁ θεὸς καὶ διασκορπισθήτωσαν οἱ ἐχθροὶ αὐτοῦ. This ἀνάστασις, says Theodoret, signifies the Resurrection of Christ. In this His enemies were scattered.

For "adversaries" the Coptic has ἀντίδικοι.

v. 4. Cp. Ps. lxvii (lxviii) 19, Eph. iv 9. For the release from bonds see note on Ode x 3 and cp. *Introd.* p. 34.

For "authority" the Coptic has ἐξουσία.

v. 5. The "dragon with seven heads" is Satan, vanquished (πατάσσειν is the verb preserved in the Coptic version) by Christ through the Divine power, when He descended into Hades, and conquered again and again in the baptismal waters.

Thus "collidatur caput draconis illius homicidae subter signaculum crucis" is a petition just before the *insufflatio* upon the baptismal waters in the *Ordo* already cited, of Severus of Antioch. Similar phrases occur again and again in the Eastern baptismal rites**. In an Epiphany Hymn ascribed to Severus, we find the following: "[Christ] wished by His baptism to open before us an ascent leading up to heaven, and to lay in advance a sure foundation for the gift of adoption, and to bring the Holy Spirit upon flesh and to crush the head of the evil one, the suprasensual serpent, upon the waters††." Cyril of

---

* *Hom.* "On our Lord," i. 1, 2.   † *Nisibene Hymns*, LXV. 2.
‡ i. 28.   § See *Introduction*, p. 32.
‖ See Denzinger, *l.c.* i. 205, 228, 275, 394.

¶ Printed in Cabrol's *Dict. Arch. Chrét.* i. 3139 from a Greco-Arabic Euchologion published by Dmitrievsky.

** Denzinger, *l.c.* 275, 285, 303, 306 313, 324, 345, 394. Cp. *Rituale Armenorum*, p. 101.

†† *Patr. Orient.* VI. i. p. 58.

ODE XXII 95

Jerusalem explains to the catechumens in his Catechetical Lectures* that the dragon in the waters of Job xl 23 is the devil whom Christ overcame in His baptism: ἐπεὶ οὖν ἔδει συντρίψαι τὰς κεφαλὰς τοῦ δράκοντος [Ps. lxxiii (lxxiv) 13] καταβὰς ἐν τοῖς ὕδασι ἔδησε τὸν ἰσχυρόν [Matt. xii 29] ἵνα ἐξουσίαν λάβωμεν πατεῖν ἐπάνω ὄφεων [Lk. x 19]. Methodius† says that the dragon with seven heads of Rev. xii is the devil who lies in wait to destroy the baptized. Theodoret explains Ps. lxxiii (lxxiv) 13 συνετρίψας τὰς κεφαλὰς τῶν δρακόντων ἐπὶ τοῦ ὕδατος as prefiguring the overthrow of the demonic powers by the grace of baptism. And Pseudo-Epiphanius‡ speaks of the baptismal water ἐν ᾧ συντρίβεται ἡ κεφαλὴ τοῦ δράκοντος. In the Homily of the same writer for Easter Eve, already cited, the question "Who is the King of Glory?" addressed to the dwellers in Hades is answered by the words: ἐκεῖνος οὗτός ἐστιν ὁ ἐν ὕδατι Ἰορδάνου συντρίψας τὰς κεφαλὰς τῶν δρακόντων ὑμῶν...ὁ δήσας, καὶ ζοφώσας, καὶ τῇ ἀβύσσῳ παραπέμψας ὑμᾶς §.

Again, a hymn of Cosmas of Jerusalem for Epiphany begins‖: Βυθοῦ ἀνεκάλυψε πυθμένα καὶ διὰ ξηρᾶς οἰκείους ἕλκει...Ἀδὰμ τὸν φθαρέντα ἀναπλάττει ῥείθροις Ἰορδάνου, καὶ δρακόντων κεφαλὰς ἐμφωλευόντων διαθλάττει ὁ βασιλεὺς τῶν αἰώνων.

It is then clear that the overthrow of the dragon is a figure continually used by Christian writers to express the victory of the baptized Christian. It is the familiar "beating down Satan under our feet." Originally, as in Ps. lxxiii (lxxiv) 13, the figure reproduces a Semitic creation myth, the beginning of creation being the dividing of Tiâmat. But in the Ode before us, the primary reference is to the Conquest of the Dragon—the old serpent —by Christ when He descended to the abyss, with only a secondary reference to the perpetual repetition or reflection of this in the conquest of the devil by the Christian who descends into the baptismal waters. See further on v. 6 for a quotation from the *Testamentum Domini*.

There is no explicit reference in the Odes to the rite of *exorcism* before baptism; but it is just this conquest of the old serpent, the devil, which exorcism was taken to symbolise.

v. 5b. Christ was predestined to vanquish the seed (σπέρμα) of the serpent (Gen. iii 15).

v. 6. It is not clear whether this verse is spoken by Christ or by the Christian disciple. The transition of personality must come either after *v.* 5 or after *v.* 6.

If we have here the voice of the disciple, the words "thy Name was a rampart to me" are easy of understanding, the Name being the protecting Name of Christ (see on Ode viii 22).

But, on the other hand, the idea that the Name of God was powerful in Hades occurs in a Eucharistic Prayer in the *Testamentum Domini*¶: "A

---

* *Cat.* iii. 11.   † *Banquet*, viii. 10.
‡ *Hom.* iii. *in die Resurrectionis* (Migne, *P. G.* xliii. 470).
§ Migne, *P. G.* xliii. 460.   ‖ Migne, *P. G.* xcviii. col. 465.
¶ i. 23.

Name, which when Sheol heareth it is amazed, the depth is rent, the spirits are driven away, *the dragon is bruised,* unbelief is cast out, disobedience is subdued."

v. 7. In an Armenian baptismal Ordo*, we find a prayer in which the clauses occur: "confregisti caput *draconis* in aqua...ut dissolvatur Satanas immundissimus *cum maligno dolo suo,*" the very words of our Ode. "Dolo perduellis serpentis" is a similar phrase in a Jacobite *Ordo*†. Indeed, the poison of the old serpent is a very common idea. Harris cites‡ a parallel from Cyprian: "diaboli nequitiam pertinacem usque ad aquam salutarem valere, in baptismo autem omne nequitiae suae virus amittere§." So in the Apocryphal Acts of Philip‖ we read : ἐν αὐτῷ ἰὸς πονηρίας.

v. 7b. Christ has prepared the way for His faithful ones (πιστοί is the Coptic; see on Ode iv 5), even as He led the faithful dead out of Hades, according to the current doctrine of the Harrowing of Hell. Thus in the Homily on Easter Eve, already cited from Pseudo-Epiphanius, when Hades is bidden to "lift up its gates," the command is given¶: ὁδοποιήσατε τῷ ἐπιβεβηκότι ἐπὶ τῶν τοῦ ᾅδου δυσμῶν· κύριος ὄνομα αὐτοῦ, καὶ τοῦ κυρίου κυρίου αἱ διέξοδοι τῶν τοῦ θανάτου πυλῶν (Ps. lxvii 5, 21). Dom Connolly** provides a closer parallel from Aphrahat (*Hom.* XII. 8) "Our Redeemer divided Sheol and shattered her doors, and He went into her midst and opened them, and *trod a way before all who believed in Him.*"

v. 8. For "didst choose" the Coptic has "didst deliver."

vv. 8, 9. He led them out of their graves (cp. the passage from Hippolytus quoted above††), and clothed the bones with flesh as in Ezekiel's vision‡‡. We have a like allusion in one of Ephraim's strange hymns about the Descent to Hades§§, where man says to Death, "Ezekiel has taught thee how in the valley the dead come to life."

v. 11. Christ "saw no corruption" (Ps. xvi 10, Ac. ii 27) while His Body was in the tomb. That His victorious progress out of Hades was followed by a Renewal of Creation was an early belief in the Church. Thus Hippolytus enumerates the topics of Christian preachers in the following order: the Advent of Christ, His Birth of a Virgin, His Epiphany in His Baptism and the regeneration for all men in the font, His Miracles, His Passion, His Descent into Hades, His Ascent therefrom, and Redemption of the patriarchs, "His life-giving awaking from the dead, and His recreation of the whole world, His Assumption and return to Heaven," the gift of the Spirit and the Second Advent‖‖. That is to say, Hippolytus places the "recreation of the world" in sequence to the victory over Hades, as our Odist does.

* Denzinger, *l.c.* I. 394.   † Denzinger, *l.c.* I. 292.
‡ *l.c.* XXXV. (ed. 2).   § *Ep.* LXVIII. 15 (Hartel, p. 764).
‖ *Acta Philippi* 110 (4) ed. Bonnet.
¶ Migne, *P. G.* XLIII. 458.
** *Journal of Theological Studies,* Jan. 1912, p. 301.   †† p. 93.
‡‡ Ezek. xxxvii.   §§ *Nisibene Hymns,* LXV. 12.
‖‖ *De consumm. mundi,* I.

Another illustrative passage occurs in the Prayer of Initiation in the *Testamentum Domini**. "When the Incorruptible clothed Himself with corruptible flesh, making flesh which was under death to be incorruptible, He thus shewed in the flesh of dead Adam, wherewith He clothed Himself, a type of incorruptibility, *by which type the things of corruption were abolished.*" See note on Ode xxxiii 1.

v. 12. The foundation of the new universe is the rock of the Church (see Matt. xvi 18). Cp. the passage from Hermas quoted in the note on Ode xvii 10.

v. 12b. Cp. Ode xii 11 "the dwelling place of the Word is man."

ODE XXIII.

¹Joy is of the saints! and who shall put it on, but they alone? ²Grace is of the elect! and who shall receive it, except those who trust in it from the beginning? ³Love is of the elect! And who shall put it on, except those who have possessed it from the beginning? ⁴Walk ye in the knowledge of the Most High without grudging†: to His exultation and to the perfection of His knowledge. ⁵And His thought was like a Letter; His will descended from on high, and it was sent like an arrow which is violently shot from the bow: ⁶and many hands rushed to the Letter to seize it and to take and read it: ⁷and it escaped their fingers and they were affrighted at it and at the seal that was upon it. ⁸Because it was not permitted to them to loose its seal: for the power that was over the seal was greater than they. ⁹But those who saw it went after the Letter that they might know where it would alight, and who should read it and who should hear it. ¹⁰But a Wheel received it and it was coming upon it: ¹¹and a sign was with it of Dominion and Government: ¹²and everything that shook the Wheel it was moving and cutting down: ¹³and the multitude of opposing forces it overwhelmed, and it stopped up rivers and crossed ⌜them⌝ and rooted up many thickets‡ and made an open way. ¹⁴The head went down to the feet, because down to the feet the Wheel ran, and that which was coming upon it. ¹⁵The Letter was one of command, for there was included in it all districts; ¹⁶and there was seen at its (?) head, the head which was revealed, even the Son of Truth from the Most High Father, ¹⁷and He inherited

* I. 28.
† N has: "knowledge of the Lord, and ye shall know the grace of the Lord."
‡ N has "peoples."

and took possession of everything. And the thought of the many was brought to nought, ¹⁸and all the apostates hasted and fled away. And those who persecuted and were enraged became extinct*. ¹⁹And the Letter was a great Tablet, which was wholly written by the Finger of God: ²⁰and the name of the Father was on it and of the Son and of the Holy Spirit, to rule for ever and ever. Hallelujah.

This is the most perplexing Ode in the whole series, and no parallel to its imagery has as yet been discovered, so far as I know. The explanation here offered is that the Ode depicts the triumphal progress of the Church of the baptized, which is illustrated by the image of a wheel moving onward and preparing, as it rolls on, an open way (v. 13)—the way of the Lord. The letter which descends from heaven upon the wheel and enfolds it is described as a great tablet (v. 19) written by the Finger of God; that is, it is a New Commandment. It "includes all districts" (v. 15) and upon it is the Name of the Trinity (v. 20); which suggests that the letter is nothing else than the Baptismal Commission "Go ye and teach all the nations, baptizing them in the Name of the Father and of the Son and of the Holy Ghost" (Matt. xxviii 19). This interpretation must now be justified in detail.

vv. 1—3. The "fruit of the Spirit" which is poured out upon the baptized includes love and joy, according to St Paul (Gal. v 22), cp. Ode xi 1, 2. Here joy, grace, and love are enumerated, three gifts which are much dwelt on by our Odist; see, for joy, Ode vii 1, 2; for grace, Ode v 3; and for love, Ode v 1, with the notes on these passages. The new note that is struck in the present Ode is that joy, grace, and love are *predestined* gifts, only for those who have "put them on" from the beginning, *i.e.* for the elect in the eternal counsels of God.

v. 4. For the knowledge of God which is the privilege of the baptized, see on Ode vi 5.

vv. 5—9. The Descent of the Divine Thought to earth is sudden and overwhelming; cp. Wisd. xviii 15 "Thine all powerful Word leaped from heaven...bearing as a sharp sword thine unfeigned commandment." It is compared to a Letter from heaven, an image which recalls the Letter in the Bardesanian *Hymn of the Soul*:

> "My letter (was) a letter
> which the King sealed with his right hand,
> (to keep it) from the wicked ones, the children of Babel,
> and from the savage demons of . . .
> It flew in the likeness of an eagle,
> the king of all birds;
> It flew and alighted beside me,
> And became all speech†."

* N has "the persecutors were quenched and became extinct."
† *The Syriac Hymn of the Soul*, vv. 49—53 (ed. A. A. Bevan, p. 21).

Like this Letter from the Homeland, the Letter of our Odist was written by the hand of God (*v*. 19), and sealed by Him (*v*. 7) so that not every one could read it, but only those to whom it was permitted to loose the seal (*v*. 8). The clue to the meaning here is probably to be found in a passage in the Ethiopic *Acts of Peter**, where Peter receives books from Christ "written by His holy and mighty hand...wherein were written the mysteries which the tongues of the children of men are neither able to utter nor to understand with their hearts, *except those whose hearts are arrayed in the strength of the gracious gift of baptism.*" That is, the Letter from heaven is not for everyone, but only for the company of the baptized. Only they can loose its seal, just as in Rev. v none can open the Book with the Seven Seals except the Victorious Christ (cp. also Isa. xxix 11). The seal upon the Letter, then, refers to the reservation of the deeper Christian truths from the unbaptized, the *disciplina arcani* being strictly observed. See above on Ode viii 11.

There is a similar passage in the Life of St Nino, a Georgian saint of the fourth century†. Nino sees in a vision a tall man, who gives her a sealed scroll, and bids her carry it to the heathen king. She demurs, and "then the man undid the book, on which was the seal of Jesus Christ, and in it were written ten sayings, as on the tables of stone delivered to Moses." Eight of the sayings are Gospel texts commanding or encouraging missionary enterprise, viz. (1) Matt. xxvi 13; (2) Gal. iii 28; (3) Matt. xxviii 19; (4) Luke ii 32; (5) Mark xvi 15; (6) Matt. x 40; (8) Matt. x 28; (9) John xx 17; No. 7 being "Mary was beloved of the Lord, so that He always hearkened to her truth and wisdom," and No. 10 "Whithersoever ye go, preach in the Name of the Father, the Son, and the Holy Spirit." Cp. *vv*. 19, 20, *infra*.

vv. 10—14. "But a Wheel received it, and it (*i.e.* the Letter) was coming upon it, (11) and a sign was with it of Dominion and Government, (12) and everything that shook the Wheel it was moving and cutting down: (13) and the multitude of opposing forces‡ it overwhelmed, and it stopped up rivers and crossed (them) and rooted up many thickets and made an open way. (14) The head went down to the feet, because down to the foot the Wheel ran and that which was coming upon it."

* ed. Budge, p. 471.

† *Studia Eccl. et Bibl.* v. 1, "Life of St Nino," trans. by M. Wardrop, p. 17.

‡ "The multitude of opposing forces" is a curious phrase. It occurs in an obscure passage in Basil's *Hexaemeron* (*Hom.* II. 4). Commenting on the text "darkness on the abyss" he says that these words have been the source of Gnostic error: οὔτε οὖν ἄβυσσος δυνάμεων πλῆθος ἀντικειμένων, ὥς τινες ἐφαντάσθησαν. He points out later on (*Hom.* III. 9) that some had interpreted the waters of the abyss as spirits of evil, a view to which he takes exception, adducing Ps. cxlix 7 "Praise Him, ye dragons and all deeps," as a proof that *all* creation praises God. But in the passage cited from *Hom.* II. 4 he seems to quote the phrase δυνάμεων πλῆθος ἀντικειμένων as if it occurred in the writings of the heretics whom he has in mind. It does not help us, however, in the exegesis of Ode xxiii, for the adversaries of the "Wheel" are of earth, and not inhabitants of the underworld.

7—2

In these verses I adopt some renderings of Professor Burkitt, who has followed in v. 10 a suggestion of Dr E. A. Abbott, and who reads אתא in v. 14 as a verb [*coming*] instead of a noun [*sign*] as Dr Harris does. This is confirmed by N.

The image is that of a revolving Wheel* to which a Letter (in the shape of a roll ?) attaches itself, the Wheel enwrapped by the Letter moving on swiftly and irresistibly. The language of v. 14 corresponds to the familiar English expression "head over heels."

What, then, is the Wheel†? I suggest that it represents the Church. The "chariot" of Ezekiel i was regarded by Ephraim as a type of the Church: "the faces of the lion represent to us the kings and princes of the world who have come under and been subdued to the yoke of the Church, which is represented by the chariot; or to the Gospel, which selfsame Gospel the chariot represents‡." A closer parallel is provided by the LXX. of Isa. xli

---

* The Syriac is *giglā*. The verbs "mowing" and "cutting down" are applicable to the operations of harvesting, and so Dr Barnes suggests (*Expositor*, July 1910) that *giglā* stands for the cognate *maggalthā* "sickle," and compares Rev. xiv 14 and Zech. v 2 where the LXX. has "flying sickle" for "flying roll" (reading מגל for מגלה). But the image is clearly that of the rolling motion of a *wheel*.

† St Basil has a curious interpretation of the "wheel" of Ps. lxxvi (lxxvii) 19, which, although not in the Odist's thought here, may be quoted as illustrating the vagaries of patristic exegesis. The Greek expositors interpreted Ps. xxviii (xxix) 3 φωνὴ Κυρίου ἐπὶ τῶν ὑδάτων of the Voice which was heard at the Baptism of Christ. [Hippol. *Theoph.* 7; Greg. Nyss. *De Baptismo Christi*; and Basil *Hom. in Ps. xxviii*. Cp. the use of the words at the Consecration of the water of Baptism, in the Coptic rite (Denzinger, *R. O.* I. p. 207), and in the Greek "Great Consecration."] Basil (*l.c.*) proceeds to connect this with the φωνὴ κυρίου which gave the Baptismal commission in the Name of the Trinity, *i.e.* Matt. xxviii 19. The Voice of the Lord in nature, he goes on, is thunder; and the delivery of the Gospel after baptism may also be called "thunder": δυνατὸν δέ σοι καὶ κατὰ τὸν ἐκκλησιαστικὸν λόγον τὴν μετὰ τὸ βάπτισμα γινομένην ἐκ τῆς μεγαλοφωνίας τοῦ εὐαγγελίου ἐν ταῖς ψυχαῖς τῶν ἤδη τελειουμένων παράδοσιν βροντὴν ὀνομάζειν. Basil says, parenthetically, that the title "Sons of Thunder" justifies this comparison of the voice of thunder to the voice of the Gospel. [All this is also in Theodoret's Commentary *in loc.*] But it is not every one who can claim that his voice is this thunder of the Gospel. It is only a man such as is alluded to in Ps. lxxvi (lxxvii) 19 φωνὴ τῆς βροντῆς σου ἐν τῷ τροχῷ, "The Voice of Thy thunder is in the *wheel*." The voice of the thunder of the Gospel is only in him who is worthy to be called a "wheel," who "presses on to the things that are before" as a wheel does, only touching earth with a little part of him. And so, for Basil, the "wheel" of Ps. lxxvi (lxxvii) 19 is the soul inspired by the spirit of the Gospel—a curiosity of exegesis which is also found as one of Origen's alternative explanations of the τροχός of this verse—τὴν καθαρὰν καὶ αἰώνιον ψυχήν. This interpretation, however, will not suit the language of our Odist; for while the Church as a whole moves irresistibly to its final triumph, and the gates of hell cannot prevail against it, the phraseology of *vv.* 12, 13 is not so applicable to the individual Christian, be he never so faithful and bold.

‡ Ephraim, *in loc.* p. 166. Cp. Iren. *adv. Haer.* III. xi. 8.

ODE XXIII 101

15 (a passage pointed out to me by Professor Burkitt). Here Israel is promised help and redemption, and is compared to the wheels of a chariot, sharp as a saw, which will thresh the mountains and beat them small. ἐποίησά σε ὡς τροχοὺς ἁμάξης ἀλοῶντας καινοὺς πριστηροειδεῖς, καὶ ἀλοήσεις ὄρη καὶ λεπτυνεῖς βουνούς, καὶ ὡς χνοῦν θήσεις. This image of victory is very like that of our Odist, and the "wheel" in both passages not only rolls along, but cuts and mows down as it moves.

It is curious that the image of a wheel which is here, as I take it, used to typify the Church or redeemed humanity moving onward to victory, is used in a hymn of Severus of Antioch to typify unredeemed or fallen humanity moving to its ruin. "After the expulsion from...Eden when...it had been said to Adam 'Dust thou art and to dust thou shalt return,' *like a wheel running rapidly downwards* all our race was hastening and being driven to utter destruction*." It is when the wheel is encircled by the Letter, and only then, that it is irresistible in victory.

v. 11. "The Sign of Dominion and Government" is probably the Sign of the Cross. One of the names which Gregory Nazianzen † gives to Baptism is τῆς δεσποτείας σημείωσις. At any rate the general idea of *vv.* 10—14 is the triumph of the Church.

v. 15. The Letter is one of Command, and includes all regions. It is natural to think of the Church's commission: "Go ye into all the world and teach all the nations" (Matt. xxviii 19). When commenting on Ps. cxlvii 15 "His Word runneth very swiftly," Theodoret (*in loc.*) explains that the "Word" of the εὐαγγελικὸν κήρυγμα is addressed not to Jews only but to all men, and quotes Matt. xxviii 19. The idea of the Psalmist's phrase is, according to him, that of the rapid progress of the Gospel, the thought which is always present to our Odist.

v. 16. Christ, the Son of Truth, is the Head of the Church who was revealed or made manifest; cp. Eph. i 22 "He put all things in subjection under His feet, and gave Him to be Head over all things to the Church."

v. 17. Christ is the Heir of all things (Hebr. i 2, cp. Ps ii 8).

"The thought of the many was brought to nought"; cp. Ode xxiv 8 "the Lord destroyed the imaginations of all them that had not the truth with them."

v. 18. The mention of *apostacy* as observed within the Church is an indication, *valeat quantum*, of a period when the Church was fully organised and equipped, and thus falls in with that view of the date of the Odes, viz. the latter half of the second century, which I have adopted. The *persecution*, which the Odist also mentions (cp. Ode xxix 10, xxv 3), seems to indicate something more here than the spiritual assault of the evil one (see on Ode v 11 and *Introd.* p. 40), and to refer to a definite persecution of the Church by its foes. But this does not connote any special date, for the apostles were persecuted, as *Acts* records, and the enmity of paganism as well as of Judaism was a continual and ever present difficulty.

* *Hymns of Severus* (Patr. Orient. VI. 1). † *Oratio* XL. 4.

v. 19. The Letter was "a great Tablet wholly written by the finger of God." That is, it was a New Commandment (cp. Exod. xxxi 18); "teaching all things that I have commanded you" (Matt. xxviii 19). So St Nino's letter was written "as on the tables of stone delivered to Moses."

v. 20. The Name of the Trinity was upon it, for the Baptismal Commission was to baptize in the Name of the Father and of the Son and of the Holy Ghost (Matt. xxviii 19). It will be remembered that St Nino's letter not only contained this text; but it ended with a definite command to preach in the Name of the Trinity. See on Ode viii 22 for the virtue of the Name.

There is a passage in the Oration of Gregory Nazianzen upon Baptism*, which falls in with the interpretation which is here offered of the "Tablet written by the finger of God." "Give me the tables of your heart; I will be your Moses...I will write on them with the finger of God a new Decalogue... I will baptize you and make you a disciple in the Name of the Father and of the Son and of the Holy Ghost."

Ode XXIV.

¹The Dove fluttered over the Christ, because He was her head; and she sang over Him and her voice was heard: ²and the inhabitants were afraid and the sojourners were moved: ³the birds dropped their wings†, and all creeping things died in their holes: and the abysses opened themselves and were hidden; and they were asking for the Lord like women in travail: ⁴and He was not given to them for food, because He did not belong to them; ⁵and they sealed up the abysses with the seal of the Lord. And they perished, in the thought, those that had existed from ancient times; ⁶for they were corrupt from the beginning; and the end of their corruption was the Life; ⁷and every one of them that was imperfect perished: for it was not possible to give ⌜them⌝ a word that they might remain: ⁸and the Lord destroyed the imaginations of all them that had not the truth with them. ⁹For they who in their hearts were lifted up were deficient in wisdom, and so they were rejected, because the truth was not with them. ¹⁰For the Lord disclosed His way, and spread abroad His grace: and those who understood it, know His holiness. Hallelujah.

The theme of this Ode is the Baptism of Christ, and the terror which it inspired in the Underworld. The connexion between the two doctrines, of the Baptism of our Lord and of His descent into Hades, has been discussed

---

* § 45.   † N has 'she flew and dropped her wings.'

in the *Introduction**; but it is necessary to repeat some things already said, in order to explain the Odist's language.

Before the hymn is illustrated in detail, attention should be called to another explanation of its meaning, first suggested, I believe, by Spitta†, but added to by Kleinert‡ and worked out most fully by Harris§, to whom I owe my knowledge of it. According to this theory, the key is the story of the Flood. The Dove (*v*. 1, cp. Gen. viii 8), the death of birds and reptiles (*v*. 3; cp. Gen. vii 21), the sealing up or drying up of the abysses (*v*. 5; cp. Gen. viii 13, ix 11), the destruction of the ancient inhabitants of earth (*v*. 5; cp. Gen. vii 23), because of their corruption and evil imaginations (*vv*. 6—8; cp. Gen. vi 5, viii 21), are all found here. These parallels are very interesting and probably have a bearing upon the language used by the Odist. But it is clear, as Harris and Spitta alike recognise, that we can adopt this explanation as complete, only if we postulate either corruptions of text in the Ode as it stands, or assume that certain unmanageable clauses are interpolations. The Ode begins "The Dove fluttered over the Messiah." This must refer to the Baptism of Christ. We cannot interpret the Ode as primarily a Flood Hymn, unless we either get rid of the clause by asserting that it is a Christian interpolation, or emend it so as to read "the dove fluttered down on the olive tree"‖ or the like. Both of these are desperate expedients, not to be resorted to until all other attempts at explanation have failed. Next, the clause "she sang over him and her voice was heard and the inhabitants were afraid" must also be expunged, for it will not agree with the story of the Dove and the Ark. Again, it is impossible, as Harris sees, to get rid of the allusions to the Descent into Hades (see especially *vv*. 3, 4, 5); so that the idea that the Ode is a Flood Hymn is not adequate¶. We must start with the opening verse, which is plainly Christian, and carries an allusion to Christ's Baptism.

We are not, however, to dismiss the parallels with Genesis and the coincidences of language with the story of the Flood, as accidental. It is natural to expect them in a baptismal Ode, the waters of the Flood being regarded as typical of the waters of baptism from the beginnings of Christian speculation (cp. 1 Pet. iii 19—21, a passage which also treats of the Descent into Hades). The theme here is the Baptism of Christ and the terrors which it inspired among the dwellers in the Abyss, the Underworld which is the abode of evil spirits, and the story is told in terms of the story of the Flood, when the waters destroyed the wicked.

v. 1. "The Dove" is the Dove which symbolised the Holy Spirit at the Baptism of Christ; it recalls, however, the Dove which returned to the Ark.

* p. 32 f.
† In Preuschen's *Zeitschrift*, 1910, p. 279.
‡ *Studien und Kritiken*, July 1911.
§ *Expositor*, Nov. 1911, pp. 410 ff.
‖ So Harris suggests tentatively. (*Expositor*, Nov. 1911, p. 416.)
¶ See also on Ode xxxi 1.

We have this in Gregory Nazianzen*: "Jesus goeth up out of the water...for with Himself He carries up the world...and sees the heaven opened which Adam had shut against himself and all his posterity, as the gates of Paradise by the flaming sword. And the Spirit bears witness to His Godhead, for He descends upon One that is like Him...like a Dove...and, moreover, *the Dove has from distant ages been wont to proclaim the end of the Flood.*" So, too, Hippolytus writes: "As in the Ark of Noah the love of God towards man is signified by the dove, so also now the Spirit, descending in the form of a dove...rested on Him to whom the witness was borne. For what reason? that the faithfulness of the Father's voice might be made known, and that the prophetic utterance of a long time past might be ratified. And what utterance is this? 'The Voice of the Lord upon the waters, the God of glory thundered; the Lord upon many waters' (Ps. xxix 3)"†. And, more explicitly still, in the ninth century Syriac Commentary of Isho'dad (which incorporates much old material) on Matt. iii 16‡: "As a dove first announced about the termination of the material Flood; thus even now she announced the termination of the intellectual destroying Flood."

The verb "fluttered" is noteworthy, and Harris aptly compares the expression of Justin Martyr: ὡς περιστερὰν τὸ ἅγιον πνεῦμα ἐπιπτῆναι ἐπ' αὐτόν§. As Resch has shewn‖, the word ἐπιπτῆναι is found also in references to Christ's Baptism in the Sibylline Oracles (VII. 67) and in Origen¶, and its rendering *volare* or *devolare* in Tertullian** and Hilary††, shewing that it probably had a place in some extra-canonical record. The baptismal *Ordo* of Severus has the same thing: "Spiritus sanctus in similitudinem columbae *volans* descendit mansitque super caput Filii et super aquas *incubavit*‡‡.

"Because He was her head." The Holy Spirit is feminine in Syriac literature (see on Ode xxxvi 3). Yet we should expect to have "*our Head*" here. Ephraim's ninth Hymn on the Epiphany begins: "O John, who sawest the Spirit, that abode on the Head of the Son, to shew how the Head of the Highest went down and was baptized, and came up to be Head on earth"§§.

"She sang over Him." The Voice from Heaven is the voice of the Holy Spirit, the singing of the Dove.

"Her voice was heard," *i.e.* in the Underworld, inspiring terror (see *Introd.* p. 34).

v. 2. "The inhabitants," *i.e.* of the abyss, "were afraid." It has been pointed out in the *Introduction*‖‖, that the Eastern baptismal rituals regularly

---

* On the Holy Lights, § 16. † Theophania, § 7.
‡ Horae Semiticae, No. v. p. 28 (ed. Margaret D. Gibson).
§ Tryph. 88.
‖ Aussercanonische Paralleltexte zu Lucas, p. 15.
¶ c. Celsum, I. 40, 41. ** Adv. Val. 27.
†† in Ps. liv. 7. ‡‡ Denzinger, l.c. I. 311.
§§ This is the translation in Dr Gwynn's edition. ‖‖ p. 33.

bring in the idea that the Waters were terrified at the coming of Christ to the Jordan for baptism. They quote Pss. lxxvii 17, cxiv 3, xxix 3 ; the thought being explained in Origen's paraphrase of Ps. lxxvii 17 : αἱ ἄβυσσοι τὰς καταχθονίους δυνάμεις δηλοῦσιν, αἵτινες ἐν τῇ παρουσίᾳ Χριστοῦ ἐταράχθησαν. Not only are the waters afraid, but the evil spirits who dwell in and about the abyss are scared away. We find a prayer about this in the baptismal *Ordo* of Severus*: "fugiant itaque umbrae invisibiles et aëreae, quaeso te, Domine, neque delitescat in aquis istis tenebrosus daemon."

v. 3. The drooping of the wings of birds and the death of reptiles here mentioned have suggested to some writers the destruction of the Flood (Gen. vii 21). But if that universal destruction were in the singer's mind, he expressed it very inadequately, for why should he have omitted the death of beasts ? I suggest that the clue to his language is rather to be found in the prayer just cited from the *Ordo* of Severus. The 'birds' are the evil spirits of the air, "umbrae invisibiles et aëreae," and the 'creeping things' are the demons who dwell in the dark waters, "tenebrosus daemon."

"The abysses opened themselves and were hidden." This is the literal rendering of the Syriac, which Harris emends so as to give "the abysses were opened which had been hidden." Cp. Ode xxxi 1 "the abysses were dissolved before the Lord" and the note at that place. The key to both phrases may be found in a prayer in an Armenian baptismal rite†: "respiciente te turbatae sunt aquae cunctae ; qui terribili praecepto tuo *clausisti abyssum et aperuisti illam* verbo oris tui...confregisti caput draconis in aqua." That is, the opening of the abysses or depths of Hell was consequent upon the Descent of Christ. *Patefacta sunt omnia* is the phrase of the *Descensus ad inferos* ‡.

"They were asking for the Lord" [sc. Christ] "like women in travail." The *Descensus ad inferos* records at length the cries and lamentations of the demons at the entrance of Christ to Hades. "Gemens infernus ululat," as the old hymn says. Cp. Ode xlii 15.

v. 4. I follow Burkitt's rendering : "He was not given to them for food." This enigmatical phrase receives its explanation from a passage in the *Testamentum Domini*§, which speaks of the Descent into Hades: "Death, when he saw Him descending in His soul to Sheol, was deceived, and *hoped that He was food for him*, as was his custom." So Aphrahat‖ has it: "When Jesus had fulfilled His ministry among the dead, Death sent Him forth from His realm, and suffered Him not to remain there. And *to devour Him like all the dead, he counted it not pleasure.* He had no power over the Holy One, nor was He given over to corruption." Harris in the *Expositor* for November 1911 compares Ephraim *Nisibene Hymns* xxxv. 6 and xxxix. 18, where there are allusions to the involuntary "fasting" of Death.

v. 5. "They sealed up the abysses with the seal of the Lord." Cp. the

---

* Denzinger, *l.c.* 306; cp. p. 275.
† Denzinger, I. 394.   ‡ B. 8 (24).
§ I. 28.   ‖ *Dem.* XXII. *of Death*, § 4.

phrases of a Coptic baptismal office*: "qui in unum locum aquas congregasti ac mare coercuisti, *abyssosque obserasti, easque sancto et gloriosissimo nomine obsignasti.*" The thought of the Seal of the Lord was the destruction of the ancient dwellers in Hades.

Burkitt translates: "the abysses were themselves immersed at the immersion of the Lord."

v. 6. "The end of their corruption was the Life"; *i.e.* the New Life abolished the things of corruption. So Aphrahat says that when Christ had come forth from the Realm of Death, "He left with him as a poison the promise of Life, that by degrees his power should be done away"†. An even closer parallel to *vv.* 4, 6 may be found in Ephraim‡: "when Death came to feed after his custom, the Life in His turn swallowed up Death. This is the food that hungered to eat its eater."

v. 7. The end of their weakness was destruction. The demons were beyond redemption.

v. 8. "The Lord (sc. Christ) brought to nought the thoughts of all those with whom the truth was not"; *i.e.* the plans and projects of the Satanic host were overthrown.

v. 9. They who had proudly thought to withstand the victorious Christ were rejected, for they had not the truth.

v. 10. "For the Lord disclosed His way, and spread abroad His grace: and those who understood it, know His holiness." It is only the devils who are thus rejected; for the Lord announces His grace in Hades to the saints. Possibly this last verse may have a more general application, but, at any rate, the thought of the Redemption in Hades was present to the mind of the Odist.

Ode XXV.

¹I was rescued from my bonds, and unto thee, my God, I fled: ²for thou art the right hand of my salvation and my helper§. ³Thou hast restrained those that rise up against me, ⁴and I shall see them no more‖: because thy face was with me, which saved me by thy grace. ⁵But I was despised and rejected in the eyes of many: and I was in their eyes like lead, ⁶and strength was

---

* Denzinger, I. 205. A similar prayer is found in a Syrian Jacobite office (at p. 275).

† *Dem.* XXII. *of Death,* § 5.

‡ *Hom.* I. *On our Lord,* § 3.

§ The Coptic has "thou hast become for me a right hand, delivering me and helping me."

‖ The Coptic has "they have not shewn themselves.". N has "they have been seen no more."

mine from thyself and help. ⁷Thou didst set me a lamp at my right hand and at my left: and in me there shall be nothing that is not light: ⁸and I was clothed with the covering of thy Spirit*, and thou didst remove from me my raiment of skin; ⁹for thy right hand lifted me up and removed sickness from me: ¹⁰and I became mighty in the† truth, and holy by thy righteousness; and all my adversaries were afraid of me; ¹¹and I became admirable‡ by the name of the Lord, and was justified by His gentleness, and His rest is for ever and ever. Hallelujah.

This Ode of Deliverance from bonds is placed in the mouth of the neophyte, who thus expresses his rejoicing. It is one of the Odes embedded in *Pistis Sophia*.

v. 1. For baptism as a release from bonds, see on Ode x 3.

v. 2. "My helper"; cf. Odes vii 3, viii 7, xxi 1.

v. 3. "Restrained." The Coptic preserves the word ἐκώλυσας.

v. 5. The new Christian is despised by those who do not know the Gospel; he is "in their eyes like lead." A like phrase is found in Wisd. ii 16 (quoted by Harris), where the unrighteous say that by the righteous man they are accounted as base metal, εἰς κίβδηλον ἐλογίσθημεν αὐτῷ.

v. 7. "Thou didst set me a lamp at my right hand and at my left." There is a rubric in a Jacobite baptismal *Ordo*||, which may explain this: "Cooperit aquam velo albo, et ponit crucem; et accendunt *duas candelas hinc et inde*." This would refer to a practice of placing candles at each side of the font. But most likely the allusion is to an earlier practice, according to which torches or tapers were placed in the hands of the newly baptized, as they moved in joyful procession. This is explicitly stated by Gregory Nazianzen¶, and Cyril of Jerusalem calls the torches λαμπάδες νυμφαγωγίας**. Denzinger gives a Maronite Order of Confirmation†† which has the rubric: "Et tradit baptizato candelam accensam ante altare." So Ephraim sings: "Ye baptized, receive your lamps, like the lamps of the house of Gideon; conquer the darkness by your lamps‡‡." And a Hymn of Cosmas of Jerusalem for the Epiphany season has|||: ῥαθυμίαν ἄποθεν ἡμῶν βαλώμεθα, καὶ φαιδραῖς ταῖς λαμπάσι τῷ ἀθανάτῳ νυμφίῳ Χριστῷ ὕμνοις συναντήσωμεν.

"In me there shall be nothing that is not light." See on Ode xxi 2, for the white robes of baptism, and references in the note on Ode xv 3.

v. 8. The "coats of skins" of Gen. iii 21 mystically represent, according to several Fathers, the νέκρωσις or liability to death which the human body

---

* The Coptic has "grace."
‡ Or 'of the Lord.'
¶ *Orat.* xl. 46.
†† *l.c.* I. 351.
|||| Migne, *P. G.* xcviii. col. 473.

† N has 'thy.'
|| Denzinger, *l.c.* I. 292.
** *Procat.* I.
‡‡ *Epiphany Hymns*, vii. 9.

incurred at the fall. This is the view of Origen*, and of Gregory of Nyssa†, and of Ephraim who propounds the ἐρώτησις· τί δηλοῦσιν οἱ δερμάτινοὶ χιτῶνες; the answer being νεκρώσιμον οὖν σύμβολον τοῦτο περιέθηκε‡, that is, the coats of skins, being the skins of dead animals, are a symbol of mortality.

This corruptible nature is, in some sort, laid aside at baptism, and so Jerome explains: "Praeceptis Dei lavandi sumus, et cum parati ad indumentum Christi, *tunicas pelliceas deposuerimus, tunc induemur veste linea*, nihil in se mortis habente, sed tota candida, ut de baptismo consurgentes, cingamus lumbos in veritate"§. This is exactly the thought, and almost the phrase, of our Odist. "I was clothed with the covering of thy Spirit, and thou didst remove from me my raiment of skin." We have a hint of the same idea in Cyril, who speaks of "the rough garment of sins," τὸ τραχὺ τῶν ἁμαρτιῶν∥. So Ephraim says of Christ "He was wrapped in swaddling clothes as Adam with leaves, and clad in garments instead of skins¶," sc. at His Baptism in the Jordan. And Moses bar Kepha states explicitly that "the white robes shew that the baptized...will put on the glory which Adam wore before he transgressed the commandment**."

v. 9. See, for the supposed bodily effects of baptism, the note on Ode vi 14.

v. 10. "Mighty in the truth"; see on Ode viii 9.

v. 11. For the Name, see on Ode viii 22.

Ode XXVI.

¹I poured out praise to the Lord, for I am His: ²and I will speak His holy song, for my heart is with Him. ³For His harp is in my hands, and the Odes of His rest shall not be silent. ⁴I will cry unto Him from my whole heart: I will praise and exalt Him with all my members. ⁵For from the east and even to the west is His praise: ⁶and from the south and even to the north is the confession of Him: ⁷and from the top of the hills to their utmost bound is His perfection. ⁸Who can write the Psalms of the Lord, or who read them? ⁹or who can train his soul for life, that his soul may be saved, ¹⁰or who can rest on the Most High, so that with His mouth he may speak? ¹¹Who is able to interpret

---

* *in Gen.* iii. 21.

† *Oratio Cat.* viii., where see Srawley's note for further references.

‡ Opp. III. 477 *in sanctam Parasceuen*. The "coat of skin" is the garment of shame, according to Ps.-Epiphanius (Migne, *P. G.* XLIII. 464).

§ *Ep. ad Fabiolam.* ∥ *Cat.* I. 2; cp. xv. 25.

¶ *Nativity Hymns*, xvi. 13.

** Quoted by Aytoun, *Expositor*, Oct. 1911, p. 340.

the wonders of the Lord? ¹²For he who could interpret would be dissolved and would become that which is interpreted. ¹³For it suffices to know and to rest: for in rest the singers stand, ¹⁴like a river which has an abundant fountain, and flows to the help of them that seek it. Hallelujah.

v. 3. For the Harp of the Lord, see on Ode vi 1.

v. 12. This is the true spirit of Christian Agnosticism. God is beyond our interpretations. If we could interpret His wonders adequately, we should be ourselves Divine. But Burkitt translates "he that interprets will be dissolved, and that which is interpreted will remain."

v. 13. For the baptismal rest, see the note on Ode iii 6.

ODE XXVII.

¹I stretched out my hands and sanctified my Lord: ²for the extension of my hands is His sign: ³and my expansion is the upright tree (or cross).

This little Ode appears again as the *exordium* of Ode xlii, where it seems out of place, for it is spoken by a believer and the rest of Ode xlii is *ex ore Christi*. Zahn says of these verses: "sie sind eine liturgische Formel von ausgesprochen christlichen Charakter, mit welcher der Sänger sich zu gottesdienstlichem Gebet anschickt*." This is an important observation, but the verses are used in this place as an independent Hymn.

v. 1. References have already been given (Ode xxi 1) for the stretching out of the hands in the baptismal ritual; but a further point is suggested here. The significance of this act was held to be that the arms thus extended formed a cross, and so recalled and symbolised the Passion. This has been worked out by Dr Plooij of Tiel†. Tertullian says so explicitly: "nos vero non attollimus tantum [sc. the hands, as even the Jews did] sed etiam expandimus et *dominicam passionem modulantes* et orantes confitemur Christo‡." Eusebius in like manner speaks of a martyr as he prayed stretching out his hands in the form of a cross§. And some of the baptismal rites emphasise this idea. A Coptic rite‖ has the rubric: "Deinde denudetur baptizandus et *manus erectas in formam crucis* teneat" before the Renunciation and the Confession.

* *Neue Kirchl. Ztschr.* 1910, S. 694.
† *De "Oranten"-houding in de Oden van Salomo* (Theologisch Tijdschrift, 1911, s. 449).
‡ *De Orat.* 14. § *H. E.* VIII. 7.
‖ Denzinger, *l.c.* I. 198.

8 *

v. 3. The sign of the Cross is thus veiled in mystical language, as is the manner of the Odist, for the Cross is a Christian mystery, described in the *Testamentum Domini** as "the mystery which is revealed, which is for the faithful."

Ode XXVIII.

¹As the wings of doves over their nestlings, and the mouth of their nestlings towards their mouths, ²so also are the wings of the Spirit over my heart: ³my heart is delighted and exults: like the babe who exults in the womb of his mother: ⁴I believed; therefore I was at rest; for faithful is He in whom I have believed: ⁵He has richly blessed me and my head is with Him: and the sword shall not divide me from Him, nor the scimitar; ⁶for I am ready before destruction comes: and I have been set on His incorruptible wings: ⁷and immortal life has come forth† and has kissed me, and from that life is the Spirit within me, and it cannot die, for it lives. ⁸They who saw me marvelled at me, because I was persecuted, and they supposed that I was swallowed up: for I seemed to them as one of the lost; ⁹and my oppression was to me for salvation; and I was their reprobation, because there was no zeal in me; ¹⁰because I did good to every man I was hated, ¹¹and they came round me like mad dogs, who ignorantly attack their masters, ¹²for their thought is corrupt and their understanding perverted. ¹³But I was carrying waters in my right hand, and their bitterness I endured by my sweetness; ¹⁴and I did not perish, for I was not their brother nor was my birth like theirs‡, ¹⁵and they sought for my death and did not find it: for I was older than their recollection ⌐reached⌐; ¹⁶and vainly did they cast lots upon me; ¹⁷in vain did those who were behind me seek to bring to nought the memory of Him who was before them: ¹⁸for nothing is prior to the Thought of the Most High: and His heart is superior to all wisdom. Hallelujah.

vv. 1, 2. This beautiful image needs no justification by the production of parallel passages. The meaning of its introduction by our Odist is seen, however, more clearly when the words of a Syriac baptismal hymn are placed

---

* I. 28.
† N has 'embraced' for 'come forth.'
‡ N has 'neither did they recognise my birth.'

beside it : "*Expande alas tuas*, sancta ecclesia, et simplicem agnum suscipe, quem Spiritus sanctus ex aquis baptismi genuit*." So Ephraim, commenting on Ezek. xvii, speaks of "that bird which gaineth wings from the holy water in sacred baptism, which because it beholdeth that which dwelleth above the heaven...flieth from the world by the wings of grace that it hath gained and getteth itself away to Him." And again on Deut. xiv 9 he mentions those "who have gotten them wings from baptism†." Cf. *v.* 6 below.

v. 3. That the joy of the baptized Christian may be compared to the exultation of a babe in its mother's womb (cp. Luke i 41) is an idea which I find also in a Tract *de Effectu Baptismi* ascribed to a Greek writer named Hieronymus, who wrote in the fourth century and is said by John of Damascus to have been a presbyter of Jerusalem : ὥσπερ γὰρ ἡ γυνὴ ἔχουσα ἐν γαστρὶ αἰσθάνεται τῶν σκιρτημάτων τοῦ βρέφους ἔνδον αὐτῆς· οὕτω καὶ αὐτοὶ ἐκ τῆς ἐγγινομένης χαρᾶς καὶ εὐφροσύνης καὶ ἀγαλλιάσεως ἐν τῇ καρδίᾳ αὐτῶν γινώσκουσιν, ὅτι τὸ πνεῦμα τοῦ θεοῦ οἰκεῖ ἐν αὐτοῖς, ὅπερ ἐκομίσαντο ἐν τῷ βαπτίσματι‡. If a man is in doubt whether he has been baptized or not, he may reassure himself (Hieronymus says) if he has these inward feelings, for they are the true notes of the baptized Christian.

For the Holy Spirit as the spiritual Mother of the baptized, see on Ode xxxvi 3.

v. 4. "I believed; therefore I was at rest": see the notes on Ode iii 6 and Ode iv 5.

"Faithful is He in whom I have believed"; cp. 1 Cor. i 9 "God is faithful, through whom ye were called into the fellowship of His Son Jesus Christ our Lord."

v. 6. "I have been set on His incorruptible wings"; cf. *v.* 2 and Deut. xxxii 11.

v. 7. I follow Flemming's literal translation here. Harris renders "immortal life has come forth and has given me to drink." If this is right, we may compare the note on Ode vi 10, for the Water of Life.

v. 8. At this point there is a transition of personality, and the remaining verses are spoken *ex ore Christi.* See *Introd.* p. 39.

vv. 8—12 seem to be a Description of the Passion, in the style of Ps. xxii, with occasional reminiscences of Scripture language.

v. 8. "Marvelled at me." Cp. Isa. lii 14.

v. 9. "My oppression was to me for salvation"; the issue of the Crucifixion was the Salvation of the world.

"I was their reprobation, because there was no zeal in me." Harris suggests as an alternative rendering "because I was not a Zealot." But perhaps the thought is rather of the patient silence with which the reproaches of the Cross were endured.

---

* Denzinger, *l.c.* I. 277, 287, 294, 308; cp. also p. 281, "sub alis spiritus tui protege nos."

† I derive these passages from Morris, *Select Works of Ephraim*, pp. 167, 222.

‡ Migne, *P. G.* XL. 862.

v. 10. "Because I did good...I was hated"; cp. Ps. xxxv 12, cix 4.

v. 11. "They came round me like mad dogs"; cp. Ps. xxii 16 Ephraim sings: "Let thy power fight on my behalf, against [Satan's] dogs who rouse themselves against me*."

v. 13. "I was carrying waters in my right hand." If this rendering is right, and the text is not corrupt, the reference must be to the Waters of Baptism. The Christian is buried with Christ "through baptism into death" (Rom. vi 4); and the Odist's thought seems to be that the Passion was the prelude to the sacrament of Baptism, which derives its efficacy from the Cross. So Tertullian speaks of the Passion of the Lord *in qua tinguimur*, and finds a figure of baptism in the "man carrying water" (Luke xxii 10) whom the disciples were to meet before the Last Supper†.

"Their bitterness I endured by my sweetness." One is reminded of Exod. xv 25 and the bitter waters which were made sweet by the tree; but it is more probable that the Odist is still thinking of the incidents of the Passion, and that at this point a mystical interpretation of the "gall and vinegar" is in his thought. This appears from a curious sentence in the *Acta Philippi*. In these Acts Philip is represented as saying of Christ to the people who had been miraculously rescued from "the abyss" in which they had been miraculously swallowed up: καὶ αὐτός ἐστιν ὁ ἔχων τὴν γλυκύτητα, καὶ ἐνέπτυσαν αὐτὸν ποτίσαντες αὐτὸν χολήν, ἵνα ποιήσῃ τοὺς πικρανθέντας τῆς γλυκύτητος αὐτοῦ γεύσασθαι‡, *i.e.* "He it is who has sweetness, and they spat upon Him, giving Him gall to drink, in order that He might make those who were embittered to taste of His sweetness." A similar idea appears in Pseudo-Epiphanius, in the Homily, already cited, for Easter Eve, where Christ is represented as saying to Adam in Hades: ἐγευσάμην διὰ σὲ χολήν, ἵνα ἰάσωμαί σοι τὴν διὰ βρώσεως ἐκείνης τῆς γλυκείας πικρὰν ἡδονήν §.

The "bitterness" of Christ's persecutors, symbolised by the gall offered Him at the Cross, was endured by His "sweetness," according to our Odist. Cp. Ode xxxi 10 "I bore their bitterness for humility's sake"; and cp. Ode xlii 17.

v. 14. Christ did not perish on the Cross, for He was not as other men (cp. Wisd. ii 15): His birth was unlike ordinary human birth (cp. Ode xix 8).

v. 15. They compassed His death in vain, for His beginnings were from everlasting. "I was older than their recollection reached"; as He said once "Before Abraham was, I am" (John viii 58). He was in being before the father of their race, and the beginning of their national history.

v. 16. Harris renders "Vainly did they make attack upon me." As John viii. 58 seems to be present to the Odist's mind in *v.* 15, this *might* be an allusion to John viii 59 "They took up stones therefore to cast at Him, but

---

* *Paraenesis* LIX. (Burgess, *Metrical Hymns of Ephraim*, p. 98).

† *De Bapt.* 19.

‡ *Acta Philippi*, 141 (35), ed. Bonnet. Another version has τὸν πικρανθέντα ᾅδην for τοὺς πικρανθέντας. See on Ode xlii 17 below.

§ Migne, *P. G.* XLIII. 461.

Jesus hid Himself." However, the words are sufficiently interpreted by the Passion, which is the theme of the later part of the Ode (vv. 8—18); and if the rendering "cast lots" is right, we should compare John xix 24.

v. 17. "In vain did those who were behind me seek to bring to nought the memory of Him who was before them (or prior to them)." Probably "before" and "behind" refer here to relations of time rather than of space, and mean "elder" and "younger." Christ was older than the oldest Jew (John viii 58). See the passage about the Pre-existence of Christ quoted from Hermas, in the note on Ode xvii 10.

v. 18. "Nothing is prior to the Lord's Thought," which is His Word. This is the Johannine doctrine of the Word (John i 1, 2) and is a statement of the Pre-existence of Christ.

ODE XXIX.

¹The Lord is my hope: in Him I shall not be confounded. ²For according to His praise he made me, and according to His goodness* even so He gave unto me: ³and according to His mercies He exalted me: and according to His excellent beauty He set me on high: ⁴and brought me up out of the depths of Sheol: and from the mouth of death He drew me: ⁵and He has laid my enemies low, and He justified me by His grace. ⁶For I believed in the Lord's Christ: and it appeared to me that He is the Lord; ⁷and He shewed me† His sign: and He led me by His light, and gave me the rod of His power; ⁸that I might subdue the imaginations of the peoples; and the power of the men of might to bring them low: ⁹to make war by His word, and to take victory by His power. ¹⁰And the Lord overthrew my enemy by His word; and he became like the stubble which the wind carries away; ¹¹and I gave praise to the Most High because He exalted His servant and the son of His handmaid. Hallelujah.

This Song of Hope in God is spoken by the newly made Christian. Throughout "the Lord" is God the Father, not Christ.

v. 1. "The Lord is my hope: in Him I shall not be confounded." Cp. Ode v 9, and Ps. lxx (lxxi) 1: ὁ θεός, ἐπὶ σοὶ ἤλπισα, μὴ καταισχυνθείην εἰς τὸν αἰῶνα, of which the words of our Odist are a reminiscence.

v. 4. "Brought me out of the depths of Sheol"; see the note on Ode xxii 1, and the quotation from Hippolytus there given: ἐξ ᾅδου κατωτάτου ἑλκύσας. In the *Testamentum Domini* (I. 26) at the service for the Dawn

---

* N has 'grace.'
† H has 'him,' but Harris suggested 'me,' which is confirmed by N.

there is a prayer in which Christ is addressed as "Thou, who from the depth hast raised us up to light."

v. 5. "Thou didst lay my enemies low" (Harris) is more literal; I follow Flemming's correction.

v. 6. "I believed in the Lord's Christ"; cp. Luke ii 26.

v. 7. The "sign" is probably, as Harnack suggests, the Sign of the Cross. There may be a veiled allusion to the incident of the setting up of the Cross in Hades*; but it is more likely that the Sign of the Cross in baptism is in the Odist's mind. "The rod of His power"; cp. Ps. cx 2.

v. 8. Cp. Luke i 51, 52.

Ode XXX.

¹Fill ye waters for yourselves from the living fountain of the Lord, for it is opened to you: ²and come all ye thirsty, and take the draught; and rest by the fountain of the Lord. ³For fair it is and pure and gives rest to the soul. Much more pleasant are its waters than honey; ⁴and the honeycomb of bees is not to be compared with it. ⁵For it flows forth from the lips of the Lord, and from the heart of the Lord is its name. ⁶And it came infinitely and invisibly: and until it was given in the midst they did not know it: ⁷blessed are they who have drunk therefrom and have found rest thereby. Hallelujah.

This Ode is an Invitatory to Baptism. "Ho, everyone that thirsteth, come ye to the waters" (Isa. lv 1) are words which it was obvious to apply to the baptismal stream, as is done by Cyril of Jerusalem†, and Gregory Nazianzen‡, much in the style of our Odist.

Assemani gives§ a Gallican baptismal order, in which a prayer begins "Deus ad quem sitientes animae bibendique immortalitatis amore festinant"; and in a prayer of the Maronite Syrians‖, Ps. xlii 1, "As the hart pants" is quoted. The words of Isa. xii 3 "With joy shall ye draw water out of the wells of salvation" are applied to the waters of baptism in a Hymn of Severus of Antioch ¶. So Ephraim** has : " Baptism is the wellspring of life, which the Son of God opened by His life, and from His side it has brought forth streams. Come, all that thirst, come, rejoice." See on Ode vi 11.

v. 2. The waters are waters of rest. So in a Jacobite baptismal order††, we have "Ostende aquas istas *aquas quietis*, aquas laetitiae et exultationis." See also on Ode iii 6.

* *Descensus ad inferos*, 10 (26).
‡ *Oratio* xl. 27.
‖ Denzinger, *l.c.* i. 343.
** *Epiphany Hymns*, xii. 5.

† *Cat.* xviii. 34.
§ *Cod. Lit.* ii. 39.
¶ *Patr. Orient.* vi. i. p. 63.
†† Denzinger, *l.c.* i. 275; cp. 324.

Ode XXXI.

¹The abysses were dissolved before the Lord: and darkness was destroyed by His appearance: ²error went astray and perished at His hand: and folly found* no path to walk in, and was submerged by the truth of the Lord. ³He opened His mouth and spake grace and joy: and He spake a new song of praise to His name: ⁴and He lifted up His voice to the Most High, and offered to Him the sons that were in His hands. ⁵And His face was justified, for thus His holy Father had given to Him. ⁶Come forth, ye that have been afflicted and receive joy, and possess your souls by His grace; and take to you immortal life. ⁷And they denounced me as a criminal when I shewed myself, me who had never been a criminal: and they divided my spoil, though nothing was due to them. ⁸But I endured and held my peace and was silent, as if not moved by them. ⁹But I stood unshaken like a firm rock which is beaten by the waves and endures. ¹⁰And I bore their bitterness for humility's sake: ¹¹in order that I might redeem my people, and inherit it, and that I might not make void my promises to the fathers, to whom I promised the salvation of their seed. Hallelujah.

vv. 1—6 are a triumph song by the Church of the Victory of Christ over the Devil, at the Descent into Hades and consequentially in Christian baptism. The theme of *vv.* 7—11 is the Passion, and they are spoken by Christ, as the concluding part of Ode xxviii is.

v. 1. For the dissolution of the abysses, see on Ode xxiv 2, 3 above, and cp. *Introd.* p. 33. Cp. the phrases of a prayer in the *Apostolical Constitutions*†: "Thou whose look dries up the abysses, and threatening melts the mountains."

"Darkness was destroyed by His appearance." The Coming of Christ to Hades was accompanied by a bright light‡.

v. 4. "He offered to Him the sons that were in His hands. And His face was justified, for thus His holy Father had given to Him." The words are clearly reminiscent of John xvii, especially *v.* 6 "Thine they were and thou gavest them to me" and *v.* 11 "Holy Father, keep them in thy name." "Holy Father" is a mode of address not found in Scripture except in John xvii 11. The saints have now been redeemed; the work of Christ is finished; "His face was justified."

v. 6. This is the invitation to the souls in the darkness of Hades to come

* N has 'received.'
† VIII. 7.   ‡ *Descensus ad inferos*, 8 (24).

forth, the powers of evil having been overcome. The conclusion of the *Descensus ad inferos* describes the leading forth of the saints into paradise.

v. 7. From this verse to the end, the Speaker is Christ, and He speaks of His Passion. "They denounced me as a criminal (or debtor), when I shewed myself, me who had never been a criminal." Harris compares 2 Cor. v 21, and translates " they made me as a debtor when I rose up, me who had never been a debtor"; a parallel would be Ephraim's "Praise to the Rich who paid for us all that which He borrowed not*." But the thought is rather of the Reproaches at the Cross.

"They divided my spoil, though nothing was due to them." This is the Parting of the Garments (John xix 23, etc.; Ps. xxii 18).

v. 8. Cp. Ps. xxxviii 13, 14 and 1 Pet. ii 23. Christ in His Passion did not answer His tormentors. Batiffol compares a phrase from the Gospel of Peter: αὐτὸς δὲ ἐσιώπα ὡς μηδένα πόνον ἔχων. We might add ἐσιώπα...ὥσπερ οὐδὲν πάσχων from Dionysius of Alexandria†. But neither parallel is quite apposite, for the Odist is not thinking of the sufferings of Christ, but of His *silence when reviled.*

v. 9. Cp. Isa. l. 7 ἔθηκα τὸ πρόσωπόν μου ὡς στερεὰν πέτραν, a passage constantly interpreted by the Fathers as predictive of the Passion.

v. 10. "I bore their bitterness for humility's sake"; cp. again 1 Pet. ii 23, and see the note on Ode xxviii 13.

v. 11. This redemption, as promised to the fathers, is the theme of the *Benedictus* (Luke i 68—79).

Ode XXXII.

¹To the blessed there is joy from their hearts, and light from Him that dwells in them: ²and words from the Truth, who was self-originate: for He is strengthened by the holy power of the Most High: and He is unshakable for ever and ever. Hallelujah.

This little Ode is of Joy, Light, and Truth, thoughts which are much in the Odist's mind.

For *joy*, see on Ode xxiii 1; for *truth*, on Ode viii 9; for *light*, on Ode xiv 3.

v. 2. "The Truth, who was self-originate," *i.e.* Christ. Harris compares the words of the oracle about the Divine Nature: αὐτοφυής, ἀδίδακτος, ἀμήτωρ, ἀστυφέλικτος.

The addition that Christ the Truth is "*unshakable* for ever and ever" suggests a time when the Church had begun to formulate its Christological doctrine; such a phrase hardly belongs to the earliest age of Christian simplicity. It reminds us of the Nicene anathema condemning those who described the Son as τρεπτὸν ἢ ἀλλοιωτόν, although it must be a century and a half earlier than that.

* *Hymns on the Nativity*, II. † *In Luc.* XXII. 42.

Ode XXXIII.

¹Again Grace hastened and left corruption, and it descended in Him to make it harmless; ²and He destroyed perdition from before Him, and devastated all its order; ³and He stood on a lofty summit and uttered His voice from one end of the earth to the other: ⁴and drew to Him all those who obeyed Him; and there did not appear as it were an evil person, ⁵but there stood a perfect virgin who was proclaiming and calling and saying, ⁶O ye sons of men, return ye, and ye daughters of men, come ye: ⁷and forsake the ways of that corruption and draw near unto me, and I will enter into you, and will bring you forth from perdition, ⁸and make you wise in the ways of truth: that you be not destroyed nor perish: ⁹hear ye me and be redeemed. For the grace of God I am telling among you: and by my means you shall be redeemed and become blessed. ¹⁰I am your judge; and they who have put me on shall not be injured: but they shall possess the new world that is incorrupt: ¹¹my chosen ones walk in me, and my ways I will make known to them that seek me, and I will make them trust in my name. Hallelujah.

Christ's victory in Hades is described (*vv.* 1—4); and His call to living men to forsake corruption, that they too may be delivered from destruction, is placed in the mouth of the Church (*vv.* 6—11).

v. 1. "Grace hastened and left corruption; and it descended in Him to make it [sc. corruption] harmless." If the text of this obscure verse is correct, it seems to mean that Grace in the Person of Christ, who "saw no corruption," descended to Hades, that thus the corruptibility of human nature might be nullified. In the *Descensus ad inferos* special stress is laid on the "incorruption" of Christ. In the longer Latin form of the legend, Death and Hades cry out when they see Him, "Quis es tu qui *sine exitio corruptionis*, incorrupto argumento maiestatis, furore condemnas potestatem nostram*." The phrase "left corruption" or "forsook corruption" (as Harris translates) seems to be the equivalent of *sine exitio corruptionis*, and to mean "pretermitted corruption" or "was not corrupted."

See further on Ode xxii 11.

For a somewhat similar personification of *grace* cp. Ode xxxiv 6 and see on Ode v 3.

v. 2. This is the Harrowing of Hell; cp. Ode xv 9 for similar language.

---

* *Versio* A. 6 (22). In the Greek form it is: ποῖος εἶ ὁ χωρὶς ἁμαρτίας ὧδε ἐλθών;

Connolly translates* "He destroyed perdition from before Him, and spoiled all its belongings"; and compares Aphrahat (*Hom.* xxii. 4) "He went in to him (Death) and began to spoil his possessions."

v. 3. "He stood on a lofty summit," sc. in Hades†. I cannot find this particular feature in the ordinary versions of the *Descensus ad inferos*, but it is only a picturesque touch added by the poet. Ἐπὶ τῶν ὑψηλῶν ἄκρων is the verbally similar phrase of Prov. viii 2, where Wisdom gives her counsel. The Voice of the Victorious Christ is heard throughout the under-world, and so throughout the world of living men.

v. 4. In the *Descensus ad inferos*‡, the invitation of Christ to the saints in Hades is: "Venite ad me, sancti mei omnes, qui habetis imaginem et similitudinem meam."

"There did not appear an evil person"; there is no mention of the unrighteous of old in the *Descensus*. The picture is filled with the happy saints.

v. 5. But the Gospel of redemption must be preached to all men, bad and good, henceforth; and so we have now the Invitation of the Church, which, as a perfect virgin, speaks in the Name of Christ, or rather proclaims His invitation in His own words.

With the description of the Church as a "perfect virgin," we may compare some words in the Epitaph of Abercius: "Everywhere faith led the way, and set before me for food the fish from the fountain, mighty and stainless, whom a *pure virgin* (παρθένος ἁγνή) grasped§." Harris in like manner quotes the phrase μήτηρ παρθένος as applied to the Church by Clement of Alexandria‖.

Conybeare and Fries would identify the "perfect virgin" with a Montanist prophetess such as Maximilla or Priscilla¶; but there is nothing to suggest Montanist heresy in the language of this Ode.

v. 7. Notice that the invitation to humanity is to follow the example of Christ. He "saw no corruption" when He entered Hades (*v.* 1); let man also "forsake that corruption." He "destroyed perdition from before Him" (*v.* 2); and He will bring man also "forth from perdition." The Invitation of the Church reflects, as it were, the experiences of Christ. For the connexion between baptismal doctrine and the Descent into Hades, see *Introd.* p. 32 f.

v. 8. "The ways of truth." See on Ode viii 9.

v. 10. "I am your judge"; cp. John v 27 and Matt. xxv 31 ff.

"They who have put me on"; cp. Gal. iii 27 and see on Ode vii 6.

"They shall possess the new world that is incorrupt"; see on Ode xi 14, xxii 11.

v. 11. "My chosen ones"; cp. Ode viii 21 for this phrase.

---

* *Journal of Theological Studies*, Jan. 1912, p. 302.
† Barnes pointed this out in the *Expositor*, July 1910.
‡ A. 8 (24).
§ Lightfoot, *Ignatius* I. 496.
‖ *Paed.* I. 6 (123 P).
¶ *Zeitschrift für N. T. Wissensch.* 1911, pp. 71, 116.

"Walk in me," for Christ is the Way (John xiv 6).

Cp. Ode xv 11: this Ode should be compared at several points with the latter part of Ode xv.

Ode XXXIV.

¹No way is hard where there is a simple heart. ²Nor is there any wound where the thoughts are upright: ³nor is there any storm in the depth of the illuminated thought: ⁴where one is surrounded on every side by beauty, there is nothing that is discordant. ⁵The likeness of what is below is that which is above; for everything is above: what is below is nothing but the imagination of those that are without knowledge. ⁶Grace has been revealed for your salvation. Believe and live and be saved. Hallelujah.

This beautiful Ode sings of the Calm of the Single Heart. Its language is mystical, and would give some colour to the charge of Gnosticism, which some critics have found in the Odes generally. But its phrases are patient of an orthodox meaning.

v. 3. For baptism as φωτισμός, see on Ode xv 3.

v. 4. "Discordant." So Labourt; Harris has "divided." The sense is that where one is surrounded by beautiful things, there is nothing to distract the soul. Burkitt reads: "where the beautiful one is encircled on every side."

v. 5. Harnack compares this saying with one in the *Acta Philippi* 140 (34): εἶπεν γάρ μοι ὁ κύριος· ἐὰν μὴ ποιήσητε ὑμῶν τὰ κάτω εἰς τὰ ἄνω καὶ τὰ ἀριστερὰ εἰς τὰ δεξιὰ οὐ μὴ εἰσέλθητε εἰς τὴν βασιλείαν μου. But our Odist is hardly so fantastic as this. What he says is that the Ideal is the archetype of the Real—"earth but the shadow of heaven" as Milton put it. This is the common language of all Idealists from Plato to Bishop Berkeley.

"What is below is nothing but the imagination of those that are without knowledge." We may compare Ode xxiv 8 "The Lord destroyed the imaginations of all them that had not the truth with them"; for while the Odist's language expresses the Berkeleian Idealism, his thought is probably more concrete, viz. of the destruction of corruptible things by Christ.

Burkitt reads: "where everything is above, and below there is nothing, but it is imagined by those who are without knowledge."

v. 6. "Grace...salvation." Cp. Ode xxi 1 for the association of these, and for the personifying of Grace cp. Ode xxxiii 1.

Ode XXXV.

¹The dew of the Lord in quietness he distilled upon me: ²and the cloud of peace He caused to rise over my head, which guarded me continually; ³it was to me for salvation: all things were shaken and were affrighted; ⁴and there came forth from them a smoke and a judgement; and I was at rest in the Lord's commandment: ⁵more than shelter was He to me, and more than foundation. ⁶And I was carried like a child by his mother: and the dew of the Lord gave me milk: ⁷and I grew great by His bounty, and rested in His perfection, ⁸and I spread out my hands in the lifting up of my soul: and I was made right with the Most High, and I was redeemed with Him. Hallelujah.

A Song of the Peace of the Redeemed.

v. 1. "The dew of the Lord." This, as has been shewn above (Ode iv 10), is a common expression for baptismal grace. Cp. Ode xxxvi 6.

v. 2. The cloud of peace is a guard. Cp. Phil. iv 7 "The peace of God ...shall guard your hearts."

vv. 3, 4. Harris renders: "everything was shaken and they were affrighted; ...and I was keeping quiet in the order of the Lord." I have modified the English, for the sake of avoiding ambiguity.

v. 3. "It was to me for salvation." Cp. Isa. xxvi 19 ἡ γὰρ δρόσος ἡ παρὰ σοῦ ἴαμα αὐτοῖς ἐστιν. The whole verse runs thus in the LXX.: "The dead shall rise and shall be raised up in the tombs, and those that are in the earth shall be gladdened; for the dew from thee is their health." It is quoted in the *Descensus ad inferos**.

v. 4. For "judgement" Gunkel emends the text so as to read "nauseous odour."

The peace and rest of the redeemed are contrasted with the terrors of the unrighteous.

v. 6. "The dew of the Lord gave me milk." See for the symbolism of *milk*, the note on Ode viii 17 and cp. Ode iv 10, xix 1.

v. 8. "I spread out my hands...and was redeemed." See on Ode xxi 1.

Ode XXXVI.

¹I rested on the Spirit of the Lord: and She raised me on high: ²and made me stand on my feet in the height of the Lord, before His perfection and His glory, while I was praising ⌜Him⌝ by the composition of His songs. ³She brought me forth before

* Version A. 5 (21).

the face of the Lord: and although a son of man, I was named the illuminated one, the son of God: ⁴while I praised among the praising ones, and great was I among the mighty ones. ⁵For according to the greatness of the Most High She made me: and according to His own newness has He renewed me; and He anointed me from His own perfection: ⁶and I became one of His neighbours; and my mouth was opened, like a cloud of dew; ⁷and my heart poured out as it were a gushing stream of righteousness, ⁸and my access ⌜to Him⌝ was in peace; and I was established by the Spirit of His government. Hallelujah.

A Song of the baptized Christian.

v. 1. "I rested on the Spirit of the Lord." Cp. Ode xx 8 "recline on His rest," and see the note on Ode iii 6 for *rest* as the baptismal consummation.

"She (sc. the Spirit) raised me on high: and made me stand on my feet in the height of the Lord." Cp. Eph. ii 6, and compare, for the feminine form, the next verse.

v. 3. "[The Spirit] brought me forth." In Syriac literature, it was customary to speak of the Spirit as feminine* (cp. Ode xix 4). Ephraim, commenting on Gen. i 2, says that this passage was intended to furnish a type of baptism, which was, by means of the Spirit's brooding over the water, to gender children of God (Opp. Syr. i. 118) †. And in one of his hymns ‡ he develops the same thought: "The Holy Spirit has brooded in baptism, and mystically has given birth to eagles (virgins and prelates), and to fishes (celibates and intercessors)," *i.e.* to the more notable of the Christian host. This is an idea similar to that which we find in several Syriac *ordines*, prayer being made that the baptismal waters "sint *spiritalis uterus* nativitatis filiorum corruptionis expertium §." Cyril of Jerusalem says, in like manner: τὸ σωτήριον ἐκεῖνο ὕδωρ καὶ τάφος ὑμῖν ἐγένετο καὶ μήτηρ‖.

Hence, then, the language of our Odist is to be interpreted of the new birth of baptism, in which the singer is exulting.

"I was named the *illuminated one*, the son of God." See on Ode xv 3 for baptism as a φωτισμός, and the baptized as φωτισθέντες, *illuminati*.

"The son of God," sc. in baptism. Cp. Gal. iii 26, 27.

v. 5. "According to the greatness of the Most High, She (sc. the Spirit) made me."

---

* Cp. Burkitt, *Early Eastern Christianity*, p. 89, and Wright's *Aphraates*, p. 354.

† Cp. Basil, *Hexaem.* II. 6 on Gen. i 2.

‡ *Epiphany Hymns*, VIII. 16.

§ See Denzinger, *l.c.* I. 310, 315, 318, 342, 349, 353, 357.

‖ *Mystag.* II. 4.

"According to His own newness has He (sc. Christ) renewed me"; cp. Rom. vi 4.

"He anointed me from His own perfection." This may carry an allusion to the anointing with oil, which was part of the baptismal ritual; but the baptismal thoughts of the Odist are apparent without pressing this.

v. 6. "I became one of His neighbours"; cp. Ode iv 9. The Christian's fellowship with Christ is in the Odist's mind.

"A cloud of dew"; cp. Ode xxxv 1, 2.

v. 7. "My heart poured forth a gushing stream of righteousness." So in Ode xl 4, "As the fountain gushes out its water, so my heart gushes out the praise of the Lord."

Ode XXXVII.

¹I stretched out my hands to my Lord: and to the Most High I raised my voice: ²and I spake with the lips of my heart; and He heard me, when my voice reached Him: ³His answer came to me, and gave me the fruits of my labours; ⁴and it gave me rest by the grace of the Lord. Hallelujah.

v. 1. See on Ode xxi 1.

v. 2. Cp. Ode xxi 7 "my heart...arose upon my lips."

v. 4. See on Ode iii 6 for the baptismal rest—the rest of the Christian soul.

Ode XXXVIII.

¹I went up to the light of truth as if into a chariot: ²and the Truth took me and led me: and carried me across pits and gullies; and from the rocks and the waves it preserved me: ³and it became to me a haven of salvation: and set me on the arms* of immortal life: ⁴and it went with me and made me rest, and suffered me not to wander, because it was the Truth; ⁵and I ran no risk, because I walked with Him; ⁶and I did not make an error in anything because I obeyed the Truth. ⁷For Error flees away from it, and meets it not: but the Truth proceeds in the right path, and ⁸whatever I did not know, it made clear to me, all the poisons of error, and the plagues of death which they think to be sweetness: ⁹and I saw the Corrupter of corruption, when the bride who is corrupted was adorned; and the bridegroom who corrupts and is corrupted; ¹⁰and I asked the Truth, 'Who are these?'; and

* N has 'steps' *or*, 'ladder.'

He said to me, This is the Deceiver and the Error: ⁱⁱand they resemble the Beloved and His Bride: and they lead astray and corrupt the world: ¹²and they invite many to the banquet, ¹³and give them to drink of the wine of their intoxication, and they vomit up their wisdom and knowledge, and ⌜so they⌝ make them without intelligence; ¹⁴and then they leave them; and then these go about like madmen corrupting: seeing that they are without heart, nor do they seek for it. ¹⁵And I was made wise so as not to fall into the hands of the Deceiver; and I congratulated myself because the Truth went with me, ¹⁶and I was established and lived and was redeemed, ¹⁷and my foundations were laid on the hand of the Lord: because He established me. ¹⁸For He set the root and watered it and fixed it and blessed it; and its fruits are for ever. ¹⁹It struck deep and sprung up and spread out, and was enlarged; ²⁰and the Lord alone was glorified in His planting and in His husbandry: by His care and by the blessing of His lips, ²¹by the beautiful planting of His right hand: and by the splendour of His planting, and by the thought of His mind. Hallelujah.

This difficult Ode begins with the idea of the Church, into which the Christian is introduced by baptism, as the Ark of Salvation and the Haven of Rest (vv. 1—4). The Truth steers its course and keeps it in the right way (vv. 5—7). The Odist has by this time forgotten the metaphor with which he began; and we have next a description of Error and its dangers, in language like that of the Apocalypse (vv. 8—14). From these dangers the Christian soul is saved by the Truth, and it brings forth fruit like a tree by the waterside (vv. 15 to end).

v. 1. The expression "I went up" would be, as Harris points out*, good Syriac for going on board a ship; and hence the word "chariot" challenges attention. It is clear that a chariot, in the ordinary sense, does not traverse the waves, nor is it in danger from rocks, nor could it fitly be spoken of as a "haven." But there is a passage in Ephraim's metrical works†, in which the word "chariot"‡ is used for Noah's Ark, and in which the language is very like that of our Odist. It is as follows (I cite the translation in Dr Gwynn's edition§): "Lo, all the billows trouble me; and thou hast given favour to the ark; for waves alone encompassed it, mounds and weapons and waves encircle me.... It in thy love subdued the waves; I, in thy wrath,

---

* *Expositor*, July 1911. † *Nisibene Hymns*, I. 4.

‡ Our Odist uses the word *mărkăbhtā*; Ephraim has *r'khūbhā*, which is from the same root (*rkhbh*), and may signify any kind of vehicle.

§ *Nicene and Post Nicene Fathers*, XIII. 167.

am left desolate among the weapons; the flood bore it, the river threatens me. O Helmsman of that ark, be my pilot on the dry land! To it thou gavest rest in the haven of a mountain; to me give thou *rest* also *in the haven* of thy walls.... Noah overcame the waves of lust...*his chariot subdued the ridge of the waves**." In the next paragraph Ephraim speaks of baptism and of the waves of destruction which threaten the soul. For Ephraim, then, the "chariot" is the Ark of the Church, which is steered by Christ through "the waves of this troublesome world," and which is a haven of salvation in which the soul can find rest. This is exactly the conception of our Odist.

Cyril of Jerusalem, in like manner, speaks of baptism as ὄχημα πρὸς οὐρανόν†; and he describes Christ in another place‡ as ὁ τῶν ὑδάτων ἡνίοχος "the charioteer of the waters."

The image of the Church as a ship is, of course, familiar. Hippolytus brings in the idea that it is tempest-tossed: "We who hope for the Son of God are persecuted and trodden down by those unbelievers. For...the sea is the world in which the Church is set, like a ship tossed in the deep, but not destroyed; for she has with her the skilled pilot, Christ§." A similar passage is found in Tertullian (*de Bapt.* 12). Ephraim compares baptism to "a ship which cannot sink‖."

The region into which the baptized Christian is introduced is a region of *light* and *truth*. See notes on Odes xv 3 and viii 9, for these conceptions, here united as in Ps. xliii 3.

v. 2. For the leading of Truth cp. Ode xvii 5 "The thought of Truth led me on, and I walked after it and did not wander."

v. 3. "It became to me a haven of salvation." Harris suggests¶ a correction of the text (due to a supposed confusion of אִיתִי *there was* for אַיְתִי *he brought*), according to which we should render "it brought me to the haven of salvation." But this is unnecessary, for it is the ark of the Church itself which is the haven, to our Odist, as to Ephraim in the passage already cited. Harris provides a good parallel here from the Nestorian Ritual for the Epiphany**: "*Save me, O God, by thy Name* (Ps. liv 1). In the hidden valleys of the world thou walkest as in the sea. O thou who art unbaptized, hasten to come to the glorious haven of baptism....*And He led them to the haven where they would be* (Ps. cvii 30). To the covenant of the haven of life we have come; to the glorious resurrection of Christ our Saviour."

v. 4. "It made me rest." Harris thinks¶ that the idea of the Ark has suggested Noah, whose name means *rest*, to the Odist (cp. Gen. v 29 ἐπωνό-

---

* Bickell renders these last words *fluctuum superficiem tamquam solum ascendit*, i.e. Noah "mounted on the surface of the waves as on the ground," making r'khubha the object, not the subject, of the sentence, interpolating *tamquam* and neglecting the possessive suffix *his* (r'khûbheh), as Dr Gwynn points out to me.

† *Procat.* I. 16. ‡ *Hom. in Paralyticum* 9.

§ *On Christ and Antichrist*, § 59.

‖ Canon LXXXI. (Burgess, *Metrical Hymns of Ephraim*, p. 41).

¶ *Expositor*, July 1911. ** Conybeare and Maclean, p. 335.

ODE XXXVIII

μασεν τὸ ὄνομα αὐτοῦ Νῶε λέγων Οὗτος διαναπαύσει ἡμᾶς). This is possible, but in any case the idea of the baptismal rest is frequent in the Odes. See on Ode iii 6.

"It suffered me not to wander"; cp. Ode xvii 5.

v. 5. "I walked with Him." Here again Harris finds a reference to Noah who "walked with God" (Gen. vi 9). If this were certain, it would involve acquaintance with the *Hebrew* text (for the LXX. translates τῷ θεῷ εὐηρέστησεν Νῶε), and so it would point to the Aramaic origin of the Odes, or at any rate to the Syrian nationality of their author. This latter conclusion may be the true one (see *Introd.* p. 10); but the premise here is a little precarious, for it is doubtful if the Odist has the patriarch Noah in his mind.

v. 6. Harris compares Gen. vi 22.

v. 8. Truth makes clear the poisons of error and "the plagues of death which they think to be sweetness." Harris renders thus in his second edition, but his original rendering "the plagues which announce the fear of death" may be right. The words would then, perhaps, carry an allusion to the plagues of Rev. xvi which precede the Vision of the Harlot. Labourt emends the text and translates "les poisons de l'erreur et les supplices des condamnés et l'horreur même de la mort."

v. 9. "I saw the Corrupter of corruption, when the bride who is corrupted was adorned: and the bridegroom who corrupts and is corrupted."

vv. 10, 11. We may well ask, with the Odist, "Who are these?", but he gives the answer "The Deceiver and the Error, who resemble* the Beloved and His Bride." The Beloved must be Christ, and His Bride the Church. And over against these are set their counterfeits, Antichrist and the harlot woman "arrayed in purple and scarlet, decked with gold and precious stones" (Rev. xvii 4). Antichrist is "the bridegroom who corrupts and is corrupted" (*v.* 9), the Deceiver (*v.* 10; cp. 2 John 7); and his ally is Error, typified by the Harlot gaily adorned. The contrast is like that of the Apocalypse, ἡ νύμφη καὶ τὸ ἀρνίον on the one hand, ἡ πόρνη καὶ τὸ θηρίον on the other; Christ with His Church, which is the Truth; and Antichrist with his companion, Error.

The larger part of Cyril's Fifteenth Catechetical Lecture is taken up with warnings against Antichrist.

vv. 11—13. "They lead astray and corrupt the world: and they invite many to the banquet, and give them to drink of the wine of their intoxication." Cp. Rev. xviii 3 "By the wine of the wrath of her fornication all the nations are fallen," and Rev. xvii 2 "They that dwell in the earth were made drunken with the wine of her fornication."

I do not suggest that the *words* of the Apocalypse are in the Odist's mind (see *Introduction*, p. 28, for the ignorance of the Apocalypse among the early Christians in Syria), but only that his conception of Antichrist and his fellows is like the conception found in that book.

* Harris has "are alike in the beloved and his bride" which conceals the sense.

v. 13. "And vomit up their wisdom and knowledge." This inebriation is in contrast to that with the "living water" of Ode xi 8 which is "not without knowledge."

v. 15 f. The joy of the redeemed and guarded soul.

v. 17. Harris suggests an emendation of the text here*: viz. "The planting *of the vine-stock* was appointed by the Lord, because he had planted it." His theory—only put forward tentatively—is that the later part of the Ode contains an *apologia* for Noah and for the planting of the vine. Noah was not really intoxicated, and the vine is the gift of God. This seems to be over-subtle.

v. 18. For the "fruit bearing" of the baptized, see on Ode viii 3.

v. 20. "Glorified in His planting," *i.e.* in His faithful ones who were to be called "trees of righteousness, the planting of the Lord, that He might be glorified" (Isa. lxi 3). On Ode iv 1 I have already quoted the prayer for Catechumens from a baptismal *Ordo*: "*planta eos* in monte haereditatis tuae†."

v. 21. "Splendour of His planting." So Schultess and Labourt.

Ode XXXIX.

¹Great rivers are the power of the Lord: ²and they carry headlong those who despise Him: and entangle their paths: ³and they sweep away their fords, and catch their bodies, and destroy their lives. ⁴For they are more swift than lightning and more rapid, and those who cross them in faith are not moved; ⁵and those who walk on them without blemish shall not be afraid. ⁶For the Sign in them is the Lord; and the sign is the way of those who cross in the name of the Lord; ⁷put on, therefore, the name of the Most High, and know Him: and you shall cross without danger, for the rivers will be subject to you. ⁸The Lord has bridged them by His word; and He walked and crossed them on foot: ⁹and His footprints stand ⌜firm⌝ on the water, and are not injured; they are as firm as a (piece of) wood‡ that is truly set up. ¹⁰And the waves were lifted up on this side and on that, but the footsteps of our Lord Christ stand firm and are not obliterated and are not defaced. ¹¹And a way has been appointed for those who cross after Him and for those who adhere to the course of faith in Him and worship His name. Hallelujah.

* *Expositor*, Nov. 1911, p. 409.
† See p. 51.
‡ This is Connolly's rendering.

ODES XXXVIII—XXXIX 127

The key to this Ode is the description in the Book of Joshua of the Passage of the Jordan, by which the people entered into the Land of Promise. Those who follow their leader Christ through the baptismal waters need not fear. Where He has gone, they may follow.

vv. 1—4. The baptismal waters, like the Jordan torrent, may sweep away the unwary or fearful in heart.

v. 5. But the faithful need not be afraid. Cp. Ambrose on the Passage of the Jordan*: "Tunc in fluctibus undarum *solidavit semitam*, modo in lavacro fidei *vestigia corroborat* (cp. *v.* 9), per quam fidem, sicut filii Israel, qui *intrepidus* ambulaverit, persecutorem Ægyptium *non timebit*" (cp. *vv.* 4, 5).

v. 6. The Sign is that of Christ. "Let thy Cross become a secure passage" Ephraim sings†. For the virtue of the Name see on Ode viii 22.

v. 7. "Put on the Name of the Lord," sc. in baptism.

v. 8. That Joshua at the Passage of the Jordan was a type of a greater Leader, who leads to the true Land of Promise through the baptismal waters, is the thought of several Fathers. So Tertullian finds in Joshua at this crisis the type of Christ‡; and Theodoret, who says that the priests represent John Baptist, speaks of the people following μετὰ τοῦ Ἰησοῦ τοῦ προφήτου καὶ στρατήγου ἅπας διελήλυθεν ὁ λαός§.

v. 9. Cp. Josh. iii 15, 17 "the feet of the priests that bare the ark were *dipped* (ἐβάφησαν) in the brink of the water...the priests...*stood firm* on dry ground in the midst of Jordan." Note too the phrases quoted on *v.* 5 above from Ambrose.

Connolly‖ quotes an illustrative passage from Philoxenus of Mabbōgh (Discourse VII): "like sign posts and milestones which are set by the side of a road...so are the examples and types of the men of old."

v. 10. "And the waves were lifted up on this side and on that." The phraseology is that of Exod. xiv 22, where the theme is the Passage of the Red Sea at the Exodus. But that it is rather the Crossing of the Jordan under Joshua that the Odist recalls, appears from the next words "But the footprints of our Lord Christ stand firm (see *v.* 9) and are not obliterated and are not defaced." In the O.T. story "the place where the feet of the priests stood" was marked by twelve stones¶, so that it should not be forgotten; and both Tertullian** and Gregory of Nyssa†† find in these twelve stones a foreshadowing of the Twelve Apostles, the ministers of baptism.

v. 11. So it is that "a way has been appointed for those who cross after Him."

Cp. Odes iv 5 and viii 12 for the 'faith' of the baptized.

---

* *Sermo* XII. 5 (*de Epiph.* v.).
† *Paraenesis* LXV. (Burgess, *Metrical Hymns of Ephraim*, p. 75).
‡ *Adv. Iudaeos* 9. § *Quaest. in Iesum Nave.*
‖ *Journal of Theological Studies*, Jan. 1912, p. 304.
¶ Josh. iv 9. ** *Adv. Marcion.* IV. 13.
†† *De Baptismo.*

Ode XL.

¹As the honey distils from the comb of the bees, ²and the milk flows from the woman that loves her children; ³so also is my hope on Thee, my God. ⁴As the fountain gushes out its water, ⁵so my heart gushes out the praise of the Lord and my lips utter praise to Him, and my tongue His psalms*. ⁶And my face exults with His gladness, and my spirit exults in His love, and my soul shines in Him: ⁷and reverence confides in Him; and redemption in Him stands assured: ⁸and His profit is immortal life, and those who participate in it are incorrupt. Hallelujah.

The Soul a Fountain of Praise.
v. 3. Cp. Ode v 9, xxix 1.
v. 4. Cp. Ode xxxvi 7.
v. 6. Cp. Ode xv 3.
v. 8. This is Burkitt's rendering.

Ode XLI.

¹All the Lord's children will praise Him, and will collect the truth of His faith†. ²And His children shall be known to Him. Therefore we will sing in His love: ³we live‡ in the Lord by His grace: and life we receive in His Christ: ⁴for a great day has shined upon us: and marvellous is He who has given us of His glory. ⁵Let us, therefore, all of us unite together in the name of the Lord, and let us honour Him in His goodness, ⁶and let our faces shine in His light: and let our hearts meditate in His love by night and by day. ⁷Let us exult with the joy of the Lord. ⁸All those will be astonished that see me. For from another race am I: ⁹for the Father of truth remembered me: He who possessed me from the beginning: ¹⁰for His bounty begat me, and the thought of His heart. ¹¹And His word is with us in all our way; ¹²the Saviour who makes alive and does not reject our souls: ¹³the man who was humbled, and exalted by his own righteousness, ¹⁴the

* N has for the last clause: "My tongue is sweet with his colloquies and [my members] are fat with his psalms."

† N has: "Let us praise the Lord, all ye His children, and let us receive the truth of His faith."

‡ N has 'rejoice.'

Son of the Most High appeared in the perfection of His Father; [15]and light dawned from the Word that was beforetime in Him; [16]the Christ is truly one; and He was known before the foundation of the world, [17]that He might save souls for ever by the truth of His name. A new song* from those who love Him. Hallelujah.

    The Day of the Lord's Shining.
    vv. 4, 6. See on Ode xv 3 for the baptismal illumination.
    v. 8. This verse does not refer to Christ, but to the baptized Christian rejoicing in his new birth. Hence the similarity of phrase in *v.* 8ª to Isa. lii 14, and in *v.* 8ᵇ to Ode xxviii 14, is only verbal and accidental. Cp. Narsai, who says of the baptized man: "New is his birth and exceeding strange to them of earth †."
    v. 9. Nor is the parallel from Prov. viii 22 to the words of this verse to be pressed. The thought is of the foreknowledge which God has of the redeemed.
    v. 12. "The Saviour," *i.e.* Christ. Cp. *Testamentum Domini*‡ "Thou art the Saviour of the sons of men, and the Converter of souls."
    v. 16. The Unity (Harris cites Ignatius *ad Magn.* 7 εἷς ἐστιν Ἰησοῦς Χριστός) and the Pre-existence of Christ are here stated.
    v. 17. For the virtue of the Name, see on Ode viii 22.

Ode XLII.

[1]I stretched out my hands and approached my Lord: [2]for the stretching of my hands is His sign: [3]my expansion is the outspread tree which was set up on the way of the Righteous One. [4]And I became of no account to those who did not take hold of me; and I shall be with those who love me. [5]All my persecutors are dead; and they have sought me who set their hope on me, because I live: [6]and I rose and am with them; and I will speak by their mouths. [7]For they have despised those who persecuted them; [8]and I lifted up over them the yoke of my love; [9]like the arm of the Bridegroom over the Bride, [10]so was my yoke over those that know me, [11]and as the couch that is spread in the house of the ⌜bridegroom and bride⌝, [12]so is my love over those that believe in me. [13]And I was not rejected, though I was reckoned to be so. [14]I did not perish, though they devised ⌜it⌝ against me. [15]Sheol saw me and was made miserable: [16]Death

---
    * N adds: "to the Lord."
    † *Hom.* xxi. (c), p. 52, ed. Connolly.   ‡ I. 26.

cast me up and many along with me. ¹⁷I was gall and bitterness to him, and I went down with him to the utmost of his depths: ¹⁸and the feet and the head he let go, for they were not able to endure my face: ¹⁹and I made a congregation of living men amongst his dead men, and I spake with them by living lips: ²⁰because my word shall not be void: ²¹and those who had died ran towards me: and they cried and said, Son of God, have pity on us and do with us according to thy kindness, ²²and bring us out from the bonds of darkness: and open to us the door by which we shall come out to thee. ²³For we see that our death has not touched thee. ²⁴Let us also be redeemed with thee: for thou art our Redeemer. ²⁵And I heard their voice; and my name I sealed upon their heads: ²⁶for they are free men and they are mine. Hallelujah.

vv. 1—3 have already been discussed, as they form Ode xxvii. They do not seem in place here, as *vv.* 4—26 are *ex ore Christi* and have as their theme the Resurrection of Christ and His Victory in Hades.

vv. 4—14 express the Love of the Risen Christ for those who have faith in His Resurrection.

v. 4. To those who do not lay hold on Christ, His Resurrection is of no avail. He is with them who love Him.

Burkitt's rendering of N here is: "I became useless to those that know me, in order that I might be hidden to those that were not holding me."

v. 5. "All my persecutors are dead; and they have sought me, who set their hope on me, because I live." This is Flemming's translation, and it gives an intelligible sense. Harris (in his first edition) rendered: "they sought after me, who supposed that I was alive." If this were right, the thought would be that those who believed in Christ's Resurrection *at the time* sought Him; but then the words "all my persecutors are dead" would be inapposite and obviously untrue.

v. 6. "I rose, and am with them, and will speak by their mouths." That is, the Risen Christ is with His faithful ones, who speak in His Name.

v. 7. They scorn persecution, and (*v.* 8) the yoke of Christ's love is lifted over them. There may be here a veiled allusion to the easy yoke of Christ (Matt. xi 29) which the neophyte takes upon him in baptism. At the beginning of the baptismal *Ordo* of Severus, quoted in these notes more than once, the words "Take my yoke upon you...and ye shall find rest" are prescribed for recitation; and among the prayers for the catechumens in the Liturgy of St Basil* is this: δὸς αὐτοῖς τὸν ἐλαφρὸν ζυγόν. But this is probably too subtle. See the note on the baptismal "rest," above (Ode iii 6).

* Brightman, *Eastern Liturgies*, p. 315.

vv. 9—11. The yoke which Christ lays upon His faithful ones is, as it were, the embrace of the Bridegroom for his Bride, the Church.

vv. 13, 14. The persecution and contumely of the Passion availed not to subdue the Victorious Christ. Cp. Ode xxviii 15 f.

vv. 15—26. This is the Harrowing of Hell, described in detail.

v. 15. "Hades saw me and was made miserable." See on Ode xxiv 3.

v. 16. "Death cast me up, and many along with me." Hades and Death are the two leading personages whom Christ overcame in His *Descensus ad inferos* (cp. Rev. i 18).

Not only was Christ victorious, but His victory was efficacious for the saints whom Hades had to disgorge.

v. 17. "I was gall and bitterness to him," sc. Death. This is Flemming's translation, which is preferable to Harris' "I had gall and bitterness." The point is that in the *Descensus ad inferos*, Death or Satan is represented as claiming that it was at his instigation that the gall and vinegar of the Cross were offered to Christ*. He is now punished, Christ victorious being "gall and bitterness" to him. Cp. Ode xxviii 13.

"I went down with him to his depths." If we could read "He," sc. Hades, "went down with him," sc. Death, we should have an exact reproduction of a phrase in one of the Latin versions of the *Descensus*: "accepto eodem sub pedibus Domini *demersus est cum eo in profundum abyssi*†." But the existing text gives a tolerable sense, and may be illustrated by a passage quoted by Connolly ‡ from the *Acts of Judas Thomas* (Wright, p. 155): "Thou didst descend to Sheol, and go to its uttermost end."

v. 18. "The feet and the head he (sc. Death) let go." Probably, as Harris suggests, the "Head" is Christ, and the "feet" are the members of His mystical body, *i.e.* the saints; but the sentence is obscure. To the next phrase "they were not able to endure my face," Harris gives an excellent parallel from the *Acta Thomae* § οὗ τὴν θέαν οὐκ ἤνεγκαν οἱ τοῦ θανάτου ἄρχοντες.

v. 19. Christ gathers together the saints in Hades: "omnes sancti sub manum domini adunati sunt‖." Connolly ¶ compares the words of Ode xvii 14 "they were gathered to me, and were saved," but probably the primary reference there is to baptism rather than to the victory in Hades.

vv. 21—24. This is the appeal of the saints in Hades for rescue.

v. 25. "My Name I sealed upon their heads." Is this a cryptic way of expressing the story of the *Descensus***, "Et extendens dominus manum suam *fecit signum crucis* super Adam et super omnes sanctos suos"?

Burkitt's rendering of *v.* 25ᵇ from N is: "and I considered their faith, and I put upon their heads my name."

---

* *Versio* A. 4 (20). Cp. Ephraim: "Satan, who didst offer vinegar for the thirst of the Fount of life" (*Nisibene Hymns*, LVIII.).

† *Versio* B. 8 (24).   ‡ *Journal of Theological Studies*, Jan. 1912, p. 301.

§ c. 156.   ‖ *Versio* A. 8 (24).

¶ *l.c.* p. 299.   ** *l.c.*

INDEX

OF PATRISTIC PARALLELS CITED IN THE INTRODUCTION AND NOTES*

Abercius, Epitaph of 118
Acts of John 77
Acts of Judas Thomas 131
Acts of Peter 99
Acts of Philip 96, 112, 119
Acts of Thomas 131

Ambrose 127
Aphrahat 71, 96, 105, 106, 118, 121
Apocalypse of Peter 75
Apostolical Constitutions 24, 53, 64, 79, 115
Ascension of Isaiah 87
Athanasius 11
Augustine 29, 59, 88

Barnabas 34, 57, 65, 83
Basil of Caesarea 6, 24, 35, 38, 52, 53, 73, 74, 79, 91, 99, 100, 121
Bereschit Rabba 36

Canons of Hippolytus 53
Chrysostom 59, 64, 65, 66, 73, 89
Clement, Second Epistle of 51
Clement of Alexandria 47, 50, 51, 56, 62, 66, 67, 68, 78, 81, 84, 86, 87, 118
Conflict of Severus of Antioch 67
Cosmas of Jerusalem 22, 52, 95, 107

Council of Carthage 53
Council of Laodicea 14
Council of Nicaea 116
Council of Toledo (Fourth) 38
Cyprian 58, 96
Cyril of Alexandria 74
Cyril of Jerusalem 17, 18 f., 23, 24, 35, 36, 40, 46, 51, 52, 53, 65, 66, 68, 69, 71, 73, 74, 78, 79, 83, 89, 90, 91, 94, 107, 108, 114, 121, 124, 125

Descensus ad inferos 35, 36, 37, 83, 105, 114, 115, 116, 117, 118, 120, 131
Didache 24
Dionysius of Alexandria 116

Egyptian Church Order 53, 68, 70
Ephraim Syrus 10, 11, 19, 20, 21, 34, 35, 40, 46, 48, 51, 53, 56, 57, 58, 65, 67, 70, 71, 74, 76, 77, 79, 84, 87, 88, 91, 93, 96, 100, 104, 105, 106, 107, 108, 111, 112, 114, 116, 121, 123, 127, 131
Epiphanius 33, 52, 87
Eusebius 31, 109

Fortunatus 67

* A Table of the allusions in the Odes to Holy Scripture will be found in the Introduction, § 16.

INDEX

Gospel of Peter 116
Gregory of Nazianzus 19, 52, 71, 74, 78, 79, 101, 102, 104, 107, 114
Gregory of Nyssa 34, 58, 74, 100, 108, 127

Hermas 22, 37, 46, 50, 51, 70, 84, 97
Hieronymus of Jerusalem 111
Hilary 73, 81, 104
Hippolytus 31, 34, 92, 93, 96, 100, 104, 113, 124
Hymn of the Soul 98

Ignatius 29, 73, 129
Irenaeus 29, 38, 49, 67, 86, 88, 100
Isho'dad 81, 104

James of Edessa 45, 52
Jerome 47, 53, 57, 90, 108
Justin Martyr 24, 33, 42, 73, 78, 81, 88, 104

Lactantius 4, 5, 6, 8, 50, 53, 66, 83, 87
Liturgy of Antioch 63, 64
Liturgy of St Basil 130
Liturgy of St Chrysostom 61, 63

Martyrium Matthaei 91
Melito 57
Methodius 95
Montanism 50, 56, 118
Moses bar Kepha 33, 47, 57, 67, 68, 74, 75, 77, 78, 79, 82, 90, 91, 108

Narsai 50, 56, 59, 68, 70, 83
Nicephorus 12, 13
Nino, Life of St 99, 102

Optatus 73
Origen 6, 32, 34, 35, 50, 74, 104, 105, 108

Philo of Alexandria 31, 49
Philo of Carpasia 6
Philoxenus of Mabbōgh 127
Pirke Aboth 48
Pistis Sophia 7, 8, 29, 45, 54, 56, 58, 92, 107
Protevangelium 87
Pseudo-Athanasius, Synopsis sacrae scripturae 11, 12, 13, 19
Pseudo-Epiphanius 36, 38, 83, 84, 95, 96, 108, 112

Severus of Antioch 21, 22, 33, 34, 45, 51, 52, 53, 71, 73, 79, 85, 94, 101, 104, 105, 114, 130
Sibylline Oracles 33, 56, 104

Tertullian 16, 52, 53, 56, 83, 88, 90, 91, 104, 109, 112, 124, 127
Testamentum Domini 16 ff., 29, 37, 70, 91, 94, 95, 97, 105, 110, 113, 129
Theodoret 47, 57, 92, 94, 95, 100, 101, 127

Valentinians 29, 51

www.ingramcontent.com/pod-product-compliance
Lightning Source LLC
Chambersburg PA
CBHW051944160426
43198CB00013B/2291